Enneagram Type

A Complete Self-discovery Guide to Spiritual Growth

(A Beginner's Guide to Self-discovery for a Deeper Understanding of Your Personality)

Roderick Weston

Published by Knowledge Icons

Roderick Weston

All Rights Reserved

Enneagram Type: A Complete Self-discovery Guide to Spiritual Growth (A Beginner's Guide to Self-discovery for a Deeper Understanding of Your Personality)

ISBN 978-1-990084-52-2

All rights reserved. No part of this guide may be reproduced in any form without permission in writing from the publisher except in the case of brief quotations embodied in critical articles or reviews.

Legal & Disclaimer

The information contained in this book is not designed to replace or take the place of any form of medicine or professional medical advice. The information in this book has been provided for educational and entertainment purposes only.

The information contained in this book has been compiled from sources deemed reliable, and it is accurate to the best of the Author's knowledge; however, the Author cannot guarantee its accuracy and validity and cannot be held liable for any errors or omissions. Changes are periodically made to this book. You must consult your doctor or get professional medical advice before using any of the suggested remedies, techniques, or information in this book.

Upon using the information contained in this book, you agree to hold harmless the Author from and against any damages, costs, and expenses, including any legal fees potentially resulting from the application of any of the information provided by this guide. This disclaimer applies to any damages or injury caused by the use and application, whether directly or indirectly, of any advice or information presented, whether for breach of contract, tort, negligence, personal injury, criminal intent, or under any other cause of action.

You agree to accept all risks of using the information presented inside this book. You need to consult a professional medical practitioner in order to ensure you are both able and healthy enough to participate in this program.

Table of Contents

INTRODUCTION 1

CHAPTER 1: ENNEAGRAM FOR RELATIONSHIPS AND PERSONAL GROWTH 9

CHAPTER 2: ENNEA-TYPE ONE – "THE REFORMER" 19

CHAPTER 3: TYPE ONE: THE PERFECTIONIST 31

CHAPTER 4: THE ENNEAGRAM AS A UNIVERSAL SYMBOL OF AN ANCIENT TEACHING: THE PERENNIAL WISDOM 48

CHAPTER 5: SELF-AWARENESS AND THE ENNEAGRAM ... 65

CHAPTER 6: THE THREE CENTER 76

CHAPTER 7: THE HELPER 86

CHAPTER 8: MULTIDIMENSIONAL PERSONALITY 102

CHAPTER 9: TYPE ONE - THE PERFECTIONIST 113

CHAPTER 10: THE MANY DIRECTIONS OF THE ENNEAGRAM 127

CHAPTER 11: THE THREE CENTER 137

CHAPTER 12: IDENTIFYING YOUR ENNEAGRAM TYPE 146

CHAPTER 13: ELEMENTS OF EMOTIONAL INTELLIGENCE (MIXED MODEL BY GOLEMAN) 154

CHAPTER 14: THE INVESTIGATOR (TYPE 5) 161

CHAPTER 15: ENNEAGRAM TYPE 3: THE PERFORMER.... 175

CHAPTER 16: THE THIRD PERSONALITY 187

CONCLUSION... 200

Introduction

"Without data of self there's no data of God" and "Without data of God there's no data of self." We have a propensity to learn apprehend God by reading the non secular books and thru prayer; we have a propensity to conjointly know the Creator through the creation. Similarly, we have a tendency to come back to grasp ourselves each through the non secular books and thru general revelation The Enneagram offers how to manage temperament through the implementation of self awareness. It supports us in changing into simpler in our lives, and it offers a path of gap our hearts and developing personal presence.

One of the foremost sensible way that of victimization the Enneagram in our relationships reception and at work. By understanding our own patterns, defensive reactions and blind spots we tend to square measure able to become a lot of versatile and skillful with the individuals in our lives. After we perceive however others suppose and feel, we tend to become a lot of tolerant and compassionate. (And we ought not to take it therefore in person after we encounter different people's edges.)

The Enneagram describes each our higher potentials and our limitations. It makes specific suggestions for the way every temperament kind will become a lot of skillful gaga and work.

The Enneagram could be a temperament typewriting system that consists of 9 differing kinds. Most are thought of to be one single kind, though one will have traits happiness to different ones. Whereas it's unsure whether or not this kind is genetically determined, several believe it's already in situ at birth.

According to the Enneagram, each temperament encompasses a bound Weltanschauung and appears at the globe through their lens or filter. This makes it attainable to clarify why folks behave in bound ways that. By describing however the essential temperament adapts and responds to each trying and valedictory things, the Enneagram shows opportunities for private development and provides a foundation for the understanding of others.

The Enneagram reveals necessary dimensions of leadership designs and assists leaders in higher understanding what drives and motivates them further because the impact that they need on others.

Global Leadership Foundation works with leaders to:

Build their data and apply in understanding their Enneagram varieties

Understand the gift and limitations of every kind on leadership behavior and also the impact on others

Recognize however they et al. React in trying things and make development ways for amendment

Support and strengthen self-realization (increasing Emotional Health levels) through the Enneagram

Apply their data and apply as leaders among their organization settings

At first look, the Enneagram may be thought of as a temperament identification tool, cherish the Myers-Briggs profile, DISC or any of various different such tools. It's true that, like those tools, enterprise associate degree Enneagram kind check can give you with a sign of your 'type' – during this case one among 9 varieties, or styles. But a sign of your Enneagram kind is simply the place to begin on a journey of find. It mustn't be seen as associate degree 'absolute' in any manner. For an honest conversation of the dissimilarity between the Enneagram and different identification tools, see this page on Ginger Lapid-Bogda's Enneagram in

Business web site, wherever you'll conjointly realize elaborated metaphors of the Enneagram varieties.

Today's Enneagram springs from philosophies dating back a minimum of so much as Pythagoras in ancient Balkan country. It conjointly incorporates elements from early Christianity, Judaism, Islam and mysticism, Taoism and Buddhism. The primary fashionable use of the Enneagram is attributed to award Ichazo within the Sixties.

Ichazo distinguishes between the stainless 'essences' of someone which person's temperament or ego. The latter could be a distortion of the former: as our temperament develops, therefore we tend to move faraway from our pure 'essence'. Custom-made to the language that we tend to use this essence represents an ideal balance of the pinnacle, heart and gut centers – the power to draw on every of those at any time. It's the height of emotional health. Our temperament, against this, is our tendency to behave in step with our Enneagram kind, which has a bent towards one among the 3 centers. The lower our emotional health, A lot of stiffly we tend to adhere to kind.

In exploring the Enneagram and learning concerning our most well-liked kind, we tend to learn a lot of concerning ourselves, concerning the gifts and limitations of our kind, and concerning the probably nature of our relationships with others. As we've got explained earlier, none of those square measure absolutes – they're indicators. However they supply us with data and insights that we are able to then use to develop ourselves and increase our emotional health.

The Enneagram could be a classification system that describes human temperament as variety of interconnected temperament varieties. Whereas it's becomes standard among spirituality and business disciplines.

According to the Enneagram Institute, most Enneagram theorists believe that individuals are born with a dominant temperament kind who may then be formed by environmental factors and experiences. These 2 forces additionally tend to influence one another. Inborn traits and characteristics facilitate form however individuals answer their experiences, and also the atmosphere plays a task in shaping however temperament is made and expressed.

According to Enneagram theory, folks don't amendment from one basic variety of temperament to a different. However, not all parts of temperament are perpetually expressed—people are always unsteady reckoning on factors like their health and habits. As you browse through the descriptions of every kind, you see yourself in many of them or perhaps all of them. You would possibly have several of those traits; however the Enneagram suggests that it's your dominant kind that's the foremost vital.

It is vital to recollect that the Enneagram doesn't recommend that any kind is healthier or a lot of fascinating than another. Whether or not the traits related to every kind are seen as a facilitator or a hindrance depends on the individual and their culture. For instance, having a lot of achievement-focused or independent traits could also be useful for those living in individualistic cultures, whereas traits like loyalty and care giving could also be a lot of useful for those in collectivist cultures.

Chapter 1: Enneagram For Relationships And Personal Growth

Personal growth is something we're very passionate about. Perhaps the most important realization that an individual can make in their quest for this change is that there is no single formula that defines the path to personal success.

Personal growth is about becoming more capable at doing what we choose, more completely ourselves, more of who we want to be. Our mission is to strengthen individual and family life, to promote integrating brain, body, and heart. Carl Jung identified a process of personal growth that he called individuation, which is essentially the conscious realization of your true self, beyond the Ego that is presented by your conscious self. Development in this is different: you are capable of looking at your life and who you are being, I. like you who are dedicated to personal growth, and really dedication is the key. After some involvement in this as you achieve success it becomes addictive in nature. If we are interested in this transformational industry, no element is more important than developing a love of truth.

The movement took as its premise the belief that through the development of "human potential", humans can experience an exceptional quality of life filled with happiness, creativity, and fulfillment. you the tools of personal development, self-mastery is. The movement took as its premise the belief that through the development of "human potential", humans can experience an exceptional quality of life filled with happiness, creativity, and fulfillment. Personal Growth, Friendship & Romantic Relationships Here I have a collection of things I encountered and discovered while in the course of my own personal development.

This information provides the short cuts you've been looking for. Positive Personal Growth contains a wealth of information that can benefit your personal development. Some of the Consequences Mistakes are concealed People are under constant stress Needs are frustrated, denied Fear dominates Power is based on fear, not respect Information is withheld and distorted Information flow is primarily from top down Behavior is forced; does not come naturally Behavior is not consistent with true feelings, which adds to the stress Conflicts and problems are blamed on the dependent's "poor attitudes" and "character flaws.

Relationships form an important part of our every day lives. The connection you have with your family, loved ones, friends and even yourself plays a critical role on your sense of happiness and personal success.

That is how the power of Enneagram comes as a helpful tool to unlock the hidden door of truly understanding people... and connecting to ourselves and others on a deeper level.

Have you ever done something when you were upset or hurt that left you puzzled afterwards? Or have you watched as a loved one acted unusual and different... and you had no clue why?

It is natural to be living with someone for years... and still have hidden depths and corners in them we don't know about. What can we expect really? We have lived with ourselves for a lifetime... yet we often don't know our complete inner side.

Thanks to the power of Enneagram, not only you can discover - for the first time ever - why you are the way you are, but you also receive the most effective tool to see through people's actions and unlock their inner side. It is truly a beautiful gift to be able to understand why everyone acts the way they do, and reach the core of their heart.

As one wise friend always said, "The greatest need for us is to understand and be understood. Because that is the basis for true, unconditional love and acceptance."

So How Can the Enneagram Help You Improve Your Relationships?

Here are simply 3 ways you can expect to benefit from learning more about Enneagram relationship tips in your personal and business life:

1. Know Yourself and Your Powers and Weak Points

You are a truly unique human being. The gifts you bring to this world every day with your energy and presence is a magical combination of your strengths and weaknesses. We all have both - whether we accept it or run away from it.

And the strongest and smartest people are those who embrace their skills and follow their inner calling, and also are aware of their dark side and learn to live in peace with it. So the Enneagram helps you get in touch with both sides, and grow from both.

In a perfect world, you don't need to hide or run away from your fears or weaknesses. You can embrace your inner self - with all that it brings to the table. That is when you are at your highest. And the Enneagram helps you exactly with that.

2. Understand Others Around You

We are social beings, that is for sure. We thrive by being surrounded by people we love and connect with. When the inner voice in you clicks with someone else's... the sparks fly. And that moment of understanding and connection is truly priceless, isn't it?

But that doesn't happen very so often now, does it?

Actually, sometimes it seems to happen once in a blue moon when we truly and deeply connect with someone else. When you truly feel like you share the same vision, the same energy, and the same passion - so to say.

So what if I told you that can happen every day? What if you could see through people's guards and masks... and see the pure inner child in them? What if you could skip the small talk and have a heartfelt connection with a stranger after 5 minutes?

Wouldn't it be magical to go through the day like that?

It truly would. And the good news is, it is absolutely possible. After five years of working with the Enneagram, it has been a powerful journey to finally be able to understand loved ones.

You'll find out more about how you can develop that power in the next guides soon. So stay tuned!

3. Find Your Unique Pathway to Growth and Ultimate Happiness

Have you ever felt out of place - in a job, or among a group of friends? Have you sensed this in your gut that you didn't belong there... but you suppressed that voice anyway because it didn't make sense?

What if you could find our the place you truly feel "at home" - for the first time ever?

What if you get the tools necessary to discover what you are truly meant for? The career that brings out your passion to life...

The relationship with whom you feel at home with...

With Enneagram, it is all possible... and so much more.

Once you discover your unique Enneagram type, you will see as bright as the Sun what your inner calling is, and how you can enhance your relationships at home and in your workplace.

People are always searching for "the way". Often it begins with religious training and for those who are deep seekers, it moves into practices of spirituality. If you too would like to understand where you come from in your ego development, where you stand, where you go in your darker moments, where your true strength and happiness lies, I recommend you find an enneagram author/teacher who delineates levels of functioning within each type. Then take that information as a personal marching order.

As an 8, my functioning can range from an antisocial tyrant (yup, I've seen that in moments-- yuck) to a magnanimous hero (makes me feel so good). and in between those extremes are several levels I move over like rungs of a ladder siutation to situation. What I find is that the more I know about my own enneagram "trance" and the levels of coming in and out of that trance, the better I understand where I am standing on that ladder. From there I can 1) assess how engaged my trance is, therefore how threatening to my ego existence I perceive the situation to be and decide if that's truly warranted -- typically it isn't 2) decide what it's going to take to move me at least one level up the ladder out of trance. Over time this frequent self awareness exercise and this effort toward movement help me to get more and more away from trance reactions and into my authentic self using the best of my enneagram type as a foundation for authentic personality.

Riso probably isn't the only author who has laid out these levels of health. it's worth looking at any of the hundreds, maybe thousands, of more advanced enneagram books, DVD's, YouTube, etc. to see how to parse out levels of health and apply that to your own trance style. It all starts with finding out your type through books or the Internet and begin to understand that type as your default software while you watch yourself live.

Chapter 2: Ennea-Type One – "The Reformer"

Aliases: The Perfectionist, The Advocate

The Rational, Idealistic type.

Generally described as:

Principled Self-Controlled
Purposeful Perfectionist

At their best, Type One people are described as:

Wise Heroic
Discerning Noble

Motto: "I do everything the right way. I'm always working toward being good, making things right – isn't everyone?"

The Reformer in General

People who exhibit a Core Type One have a strong sense of right and wrong, and actively work to correct errors in themselves, others, and their world. They are conscientious and idealistic, and work to maintain high standards of fairness and equality in the world.

Reformers spend time reflecting on the consequences and outcomes of their actions. It is important to a Reformer that they don't act against their morals, even if others aren't aware of personal infractions. They are passionate, instinctive people, who direct themselves through high standards and principals.

Reformers rarely settle or roll back their expectations and are often instigators of social change, especially righting the wrongs of moral injustices. They may see themselves as being "on a mission" or having a central calling in life that directs their actions.

Sometimes, while a Type One person is working to improve something (including themselves), they can become overly critical. They greatly fear making a mistake, especially when it is seen by others, and they become impatient with themselves, others, or processes.

Reformers prefer to be seen as organized, prepared, and efficient.

When a Type One person can show off as being "good" or "correct," they feel worthy and loved. A Reformer wants to be useful to their loved ones, their community, and society.

How Reformers See Themselves vs. How Others See Them

Reformers have a strong sense of purpose, but they also feel the need to justify this inner drive and their actions to others. They think they are driven by logic and reason – highly rational people – but actually Reformers operate from their inner mission and seek out reasons that explain this inner drive so others accept them.

Because Type One people are so passionate and driven, they often work to curb and control their thoughts and behaviors. While they tend to see this as "moderation" or "necessary" to keep themselves under control, it can make them seem uptight, cold, aloof, or insensitive to others. While the Type One person thinks they are keeping their cool for everyone's benefit, other people see the tight grip on self-control as constricting. At times, a Type One person may seem aggressive or resentful of their own self-control.

While the Reformer Ennea-type can see themselves as reasonably skeptical – because, in their view, the world is full of imperfections, lies, and misinformation – they can come across to others as untrusting or cold-hearted at times. The Reformer may see themselves as seeking balance between inner and outer influences, however it may appear to others that the Type One person is overly concerned and that the harmony is not achieved. While the Type One person may enjoy or seek fulfillment in the process of finding this balance, it can be frustrating or unclear to others why this process is so involved or such a priority to the Type One person.

The "Average" Reformer's Mental Health

When a Reformer is at their "average" level of mental health, they may feel regular anxiety about making mistakes and keeping reality consistent with their ideals. In this state, a Reformer may be seen as rigid by others, because they hold in feelings and become focused on work or personal projects. As they become more stressed, Reformers become nitpicky, insensitive, and emotionally reactive.

When a Reformer is feeling a little better than average, they may be dissatisfied with "everything" and begin to lecture. At this level of health, the Reformer seeks to improve the world, but can become condescending, explaining to others how things "ought" to be.

Moving Toward Integration: Reformers At Their Best

When moving in the Direction of Integration (growth) and exhibiting their best qualities, Reformers become spontaneous and joyful and can shed their anger and criticism.

Basic Desire(s): To be "good", have integrity, and be balanced

Basic Motivation(s): Desire to be "correct" and driven to improve their environment. High goals, focused on acting on personal ideals. Wants to be "right" to avoid criticism, rejection, and condemnation.

Unique Gift(s): Honest, industrious, responsible, ethical and fair. They work hard to achieve goals and visions, striving to improve the world.

Basic Goal: To embody integrity through perfection.

When Reformers Mental Health is Excellent

At their best, Reformers are wise and ready to share their wisdom. They become fluid and easy-going, less likely to emotionally react to situations.

Compassionate, inspiring, and optimistic, they share mature, well-formulated views.

Their sharp eye for detail becomes a source for compliments rather than criticism.

As Type One people Disintegrate, they focus on their obligation to carry out their ideals, which can create anxiety about "perfection." Although they can find fulfillment in teaching, their personal values and perspectives on a topic can become overbearing.

Moving Toward Disintegration: Reformers When Stressed

When moving in their Direction of Disintegration (stress), the normally structured and controlled Reformer regresses toward becoming moody and irrational.

Basic Fear(s): Corruption of the self, becoming "evil" or "defective"

Triggering Emotion(s): **Anger**

When Fixated: Becomes resentful

Once a Reformer becomes angry, they become defensive and treat others harshly. Because of their high ideals, the

Reformer may become offended easily, and it can be difficult for them to calmly evaluate a situation. They can learn not to take things personally. When angry, Reformers push people away, which typically fuels their anger. This negative cycle can contribute to stress-related health problems, such as ulcers or high blood pressure.

What Type One People Might Struggle With

Type One people can suffer anxiety related to their efforts to make things "perfect", "correct", or "right" all the time.

At times, Type Ones can delay action until a situation or outcome is "right," causing inconveniences and delays to group productivity, if a Reformer is fixated on a detail.

They have a tendency to delay their own pleasure when focused on a project or outcome. Sometimes, this causes them to ignore or suppress their personal needs.

When Reformer's Mental Health is Struggling

When fully disintegrated and under stress, Reformers become critical enough and focused enough on punishment and "justice" that it pushes others away. They can suffer from anxiety or depression regarding their deep desire to "achieve perfection."

As Reformers begin to decrease their stress and focus on improving their health, they can become less self-righteous, increase their tolerance and patience for themselves and others, and decrease their judgmental attitudes.

Potential Addictive Struggles

Type One people might struggle with addictions to diets, including crash diets or pills, vitamins, and juice or fasting "cleanses." In some cases, a need for control can lead to eating disorders such as under-eating, anorexia, or bulimia.

Some Type One people may struggle with addictions to alcohol, in order to relieve their anxiety about the pressure to be "perfect."

Overcoming Challenges of the Reformer Ennea-Type

It's important that the Reformer take care of themselves. Relaxation, decompression, and processing their feelings, actions, and choices are essential to keeping a Type One personality balanced, healthy, and focused toward growth and integration.

Being The Best Reformer

Harness the best aspects of your Reformer Type and diminish negative traits that emerge under stress. If you're a Reformer, or know someone who is, consider how the following techniques help unlock and grow the best version of yourself.

Relaxation

Type One people need to give themselves a break. They work hard, and sometimes they forget to (or ignore the need to) let out pent-up energy and emotion. To maintain balance, a Reformer must relax as intensely as they work. It can be difficult to let go of the need for "perfection," so relaxation should be in a judgment-free environment.

Type One people can find release of their emotions through journaling, exercise, artistic expression, or meditation. When given a chance to process and express emotions, they may find the release they need. These breaks can be small, but any chance to decompress can help a Reformer feel more balanced.

Suggestions:

Focus on doing something beautiful – not "perfect." Dance. Draw. Paint. Sculpt. Knit. Write. Swim. Suntan. Meditate. Play a cooperative board or card game. Converse with a nonjudgmental friend. Exercise. Practice yoga. Find something to laugh about.

There are many simple things a Reformer can do to release their creative energy, especially when they give themselves the freedom to make mistakes without criticism.

Mentoring

Type One people naturally love to acquire and distribute knowledge, and when they do, they can have a huge influence those around them. The Reformer at their best finds joy in helping someone learn something new, and they feel bonded to people they teach.

Although a Reformer can become frustrated and impatient teaching others, learning to focus on the joy of guiding others helps a Reformer hone patience and empathy.

Suggestions:

Spend time with children and elders. Tutor. Volunteer. Babysit. Start a podcast or blog on one of your favorite topics. Join or start a Meetup or other group.

There are many simple things a Reformer can do to release their loving and educational energy, especially when they give themselves permission to laugh and learn together with others.

Chapter 3: Type One: The Perfectionist

Overview

The Perfectionist is a person on a mission who wants to improve themselves and the world around them in whatever way they may be able to influence it. They are unflagging in their efforts to overcome every challenge and are particularly driven to defeat any obstacle that is perceived by them to be moral in nature. They do this with a desire to help free the best part of themselves and allow it to contribute to the human experience. The Perfectionist never stops striving for the highest possible values, even if it means they must sacrifice a great deal of their own in order to do so.

Looking through our history, we can see that Perfectionists are often those special people who work hardest to make a difference and to answer a higher calling. Extraordinary figures like Gandhi and Joan of Arc are thought to be Perfectionists because of their willingness to sacrifice an easy life in the effort to do something that would truly matter.

A Perfectionist may have high ideals, but they are also among the most practical of people. Their goal is to be of service to humanity because they are committed to the notion that they are on a mission. This might be a super-human mission like the heroes mentioned above, but it also could be a small, mundane and simply mission like making their environment slightly more orderly.

Perfectionists do have a strong, well-developed sense of mission, but they also usually feel that it is necessary for them to defend their actions to others around them—but even to themselves, at times. The advantage of this way of thinking is that Perfectionists are very thoughtful about all potential consequences that might stem from their actions. They are very controlled, and often reflect for a good deal of time to make sure that they themselves comply with their high, rigid internal standards. Thanks to this habit, Perfectionists usually view themselves as cerebral and rational, who are governed by a commitment to logic, objectivity, and truth. However, this is not actually the case. In fact, another way of looking at the Perfectionist is as an activist or a reformer who is trying to find a socially acceptable rationale for what they sense they need to do. Far from emotionally dead, the Perfectionist is naturally a person of passion and intuition. He or she tends to use instinctive convictions and judgments in an effort to control and direct their actions—and the behavior of others.

In making a constant, concerted effort to stay true to their principles, Perfectionists try to avoid being influenced by their instincts and passions, actively resisting them or repressing them as much as possible. Because of this constant effort, what emerges is a personality type that has struggles with resistance, repression, and—even at times aggression. Other people usually perceive Perfectionists as very self-controlled, to the point of seeming rigid. However, Perfectionists suffer because of this misperception as they have a different internal experience. For them, it seems as though they are struggling to keep a tight lid on a cauldron that threatens to bubble over with passions and desires. The effort to keep everything down is often considerable, and they face intense fear that they will one day explode—to the detriment of everyone around them. This is the primary source of suffering faced by a Perfectionist.

As the name might suggest, the Perfectionist believes that being uncompromisingly strict with themselves, they will eventually be able to become "perfect." This will make them feel worthy of themselves—and they hope it will make them feel loved by others. However, this effort to create their own idea of what perfection is inevitably leads them to be trapped in a personal hell of their own design. From this entrapment, they have trouble knowing how to trust their inner guidance system. Nor can they trust life itself. This means that Perfectionists often refer to their childhood learning (also known as the superego) because they believe that this voice will be able to help to guide them toward what they seek so passionately: the greater good. While it is possible for a Perfectionist to learn when they are being rigidly guided by a moralistic, childhood voice, they also run the risk of being completely immersed in it. They listen to it with diligence and cannot distinguish it from their grown-up self. The key step in a Perfectionist's path towards growth is to learn to listen to the voice objectively and take from the good parts while distancing themselves from the bad parts. A professional therapist should be well equipped to help achieve this development — but first, a Perfectionist must gain enough self-understanding to be willing to seek out their help.

The connected types of the Perfectionist are:

Wing: Mediator 9

Wing: Giver 2

Security Type: Epicure 7

Stress Type: Romantic 4

The non-connected, look-alike types of the Perfectionist are:

Performer 3

Loyal Skeptic 6

Protector 8

The Probability of types (other types to consider if Perfectionist is your top choice):

66% Perfectionist 1

8% Romantic 4

8% Loyal Skeptic 6

7% Giver 2

The 66% percent chance assigned to the Perfectionist type means that there is a high chance you are a Perfectionist if you scored the high on the Perfectionist test. However, you should still review your second and third choices and the other probable types (Romantic and Loyal Skeptic. Givers are frequently the second and third types associated with the Perfectionist). Remember, if a certain type has a strong wing of one or the other, that can greatly influence how the personality manifests itself. If you cannot accept the type you are, your feelings may be legitimate, or could be a result of the negative stereotypes you have heard about the type, so make sure to explore any strong reactions you may have.

Myths About the Perfectionist:

If you are a perfectionist, you are often described as an inflexible neat freak. You may have a tendency to judge people according to high standards, but these standards can vary. Thus, if a perfectionist happens to believe that being neat is a waste of time, or that being flexible is a virtue, they may not exhibit some of these stereotypical traits.

Adjectives to Describe the Perfectionist:

In addition to the above, Perfectionists are known to have the negative qualities of being resentful, critical and opinionated. They are associated with positive qualities, such as being conscientious, having high standards, being clear, consistent, self-controlled and precise.

The Underlying Truths of the Perfectionist

The basic principle the perfectionist has forgotten: **All people are one and are perfect as they are.**

The perfectionist wrongly believes: That we are not accepted for who we are.

The Perfectionist most deeply fears: To be evil, defective, corrupt or immoral.

The Perfectionist most deeply desires: To be moral, to be good, to be whole and to have integrity.

The Perfectionist is most profoundly motivated by these needs and desires: To always be right, to keep aiming higher and improving everything around them, to justify themselves, to be consistent with their high ideals, to be above reproach in order to avoid negative judgment of any kind, no matter how small, from anyone they meet.

The perfectionist created these behaviors to compensate for: Growing up in an environment where love was given out because of good behavior such as being responsible and conscientious. In the case of conflict, they learned to swallow their anger, and as a result, are filled with tension and resentment.

The Characteristics that Define the Perfectionist

Because of these adaptive behaviors, the Perfectionist focuses on: Judging what is right and trying to right any wrongs; comparing their behavior to others; criticizing themselves and others.

They put their energy into: Suppressing personal needs and desires, maintaining high standards and being right all the time.

They desperately try to avoid: Mistakes, loss of self-control, any violation of social norms, losing love due to "bad" behavior.

They have these strengths: Perfectionists have a high degree of integrity and are committed to self-improvement. They show great self-restraint, contribute generously to efforts they deem important, and exhibit idealism.

They communicate in the following way: Perfectionists are clear and direct with black and white thinking. This leads to being perceived as being judgmental or closed-minded.

The Sources of Stress, Anger and Defensiveness

They are stressed by: Because the Perfectionist has a strong inner critic, they can suffer a great deal of anxiety when they are unable to shut it off. In situations where there is an overwhelming number of problems, the Perfectionist can tend to freeze up. They can hold onto resentment, particularly when others blame them and do not take responsibility for what is clearly their mistake.

They are angered: When things are done in the wrong manner, or when rules are ignored.

They are defensive towards: **Unfair criticism.**

Their anger and defensiveness are characterized by: Repressed resentment mixed with intense, self-righteous justification. This repressed resentment often floods out into outbursts of indignant anger.

Their final goal is: To accept that humans are inherently complete, whole and perfect as they are and that their value is not dependent on being right.

Suggestions for Personal Growth for the Perfectionist

They can further this growth by:

Being mindful of how they monitor moral behavior and appreciating that the diverse perspectives of others might mean that they behave in ways that seem "wrong."

Letting go of judgments.

Practicing forgiveness of the self and of others.

Questioning their internal rigidity on a daily basis.

Identifying repressed desires by noticing where they hold resentment.

Viewing desires and natural impulses as positive and integrating them into their life.

Making sure to schedule free time during which priorities can freely surface, including longer get-away periods.

Getting factual information to avoid unfounded worry. Learning how to request and to receive gratification.

Their biggest obstacle is: A tendency towards being a workaholic, which is caused by this belief that they must be good enough in order to be loved.

Others can support this growth by:

Encouraging a perfectionist to spend time on self-care.

Providing them with a compassionate perspective.

Kindly observing and pointing out when the word "should" appear in their speech.

Famous Perfectionists

(including many philosophers, leaders, musicians, politicians, and actors):

Helen Hunt, Harrison Ford, Maggie Smith, William F. Buckley, Jerry Seinfeld, Keith Olbermann, Vanessa Redgrave, Julie Andrews, Emma Thompson, Meryl Streep, Tina Fey, Katherine Hepburn, George F. Will, Bill Moyers, Noam Chomsky, Osama bin Laden, George Bernard Shaw, Thoreau, Rudy Giuliani, Elliot Spitzer, Joan Baez, Celine Dion, Ralph Nader, Hilary Clinton, Justice Sandra Day O'Connor, Al Gore, Dr. Jack Kevorkian, Martha Stewart, Prince Charles, Duchess of Cambridge, Margaret

Thatcher, Jimmy Carter, Michelle Obama, Confucius, Plato, Joan of Arc, Sir Thomas More, Mahatma Gandhi, Pope John Paul II, and Nelson Mandela.

Related Types

Every personality type is influenced by the wings to the point that they might blend into one of them. If a personality type has a strong wing, it will make a huge impact on the individual's personality.

Wings: If you are a one with a more developed two wing, you tend to be less cold and more helpful. If you are a one with a more developed nine wing, you tend to be less warm, but also more tranquil and even detached.

Security Type (Epicure 7): When a Perfectionist moves towards the positive side of seven, they are able to be more accepting of themselves and others, enjoy life more, and act with more spontaneity and joy. When a Perfectionist moves towards the negative side of seven, they might lean towards substance abuse or other negative behavior.

Stress Type (Romantic 4): When a Perfectionist moves towards the positive side of four, they are able to access their repressed feelings and access more creativity. The negative side of four can cause the Perfectionist to become depressed and feel hopeless about what they do not have.

Overlaps Between the Perfectionist and Other Non-connected Types

The Performer 3: The Performer and Perfectionist both place a high value on goal-oriented activities and share a tendency to place work above all else. However, whereas the Perfectionist suffers because of a harsh inner critic, the Performer might look for short cuts in order to get ahead.

The Romantic 4: These two types are closely related because the Perfectionist is the security type of the Romantic and the Romantic is the stress type of the

Perfectionist. These types are both very expressive of idealism, as well as a commitment to improving themselves. However, the Perfectionist is different because their idealism is all geared towards "getting it right" but the Romantic is driven by obtaining fulfillment. Another big difference has to do with the fact that Romantics can be self-absorbed and drown in their emotions. Perfectionists are, instead, much more repressed.

The Loyal Skeptic 6: These two types can be similar because both feel high levels of anxiety as they try to understand the world around them. The main difference is that the Loyal Skeptic over-analyzes in a search for security while the Perfectionist does so in order to avoid negative judgment.

The Protector 8: Both types belong to the body center and, therefore, are focused on truth and justice. Whereas Protectors are comfortable venting their anger and quickly spring into action, Perfectionists are masters at suppressing their anger until it eventually boils over.

The Mediator 9: Both types belong to the same body center, which is why they have so much in common. They both are easily able to suppress their desires in order to get what they truly value. Both types also value routine and hard work. However, whereas Perfectionists are rigid in their ideals, Mediators are flexible (sometimes overly so).

Chapter 4: The Enneagram As A Universal Symbol Of An Ancient Teaching: The Perennial Wisdom

There is one thing about the enneagram that makes it such a useful tool. It is a tangible form of humanity's common ground – our shared human experience. Everyone sees the world differently and the enneagram helps us recognize this and understand others better.

Whereas in the previous chapter, the science of personality was discussed, this time, we're going to dive into the spiritual side of things. They do not always have to be completely separate. The enneagram can bridge the gap between psychology and spirituality.

History of the Enneagram

It's important to take a look at the Enneagram's history to understand how its use has changed throughout the years.

Until today, the origins of the Enneagram of Personality is in dispute. Writers such as Wiltse and Palmer posited that as early as the 4th century, ideas that are reminiscent of those in the modern Enneagram can already be found in the works of Evagrius Ponticus.

Evagrius is an ascetic known for being a thinker, writer, and speaker. He identified 8 of what he called Logismoi (deadly thoughts) – thoughts from which harmful behavior arises. He also identified the ways with which these thoughts could be 'remedied. So it's safe to assume that as early as the 4th century, some people were already using philosophy similar to those that the modern Enneagram espouses in order to explain human behavior and mitigate effects – a self-development practice.

The Enneagram of Personality was initially developed by Oscar Ichazo, a Bolivian author and philosopher, in the 1950s, although the Enneagram that is known today was developed from his teachings and those of another notable psychiatrist - Claudio Naranjo. However, it was only in the 1970s after Ichazo moved to the US to refine his understanding of the Enneagram that the school of thought gained ground and influenced others including some Jesuit missionaries who adapted the use of his Ennegram in nurturing spirituality.

Some modern Enneagram experts claim that Ichazo's Enneagram appears to be inspired by Gurdjieff's work on what he believed to be the three traditional ways of the mind. Gurdjieff believed in universal patterns and movements.

During Gurdjieff's time, Eastern teachings operate on the philosophy that that there are three classic ways of transformation – body work, which is accomplished through hatha yoga, emotion work which is accomplished through monasticism, and Mind work, which is accomplished through raja yoga. Gurdjieff proposed the fourth way – a way in which one stays in the midst of all three to find balance.

Gurdjieff did not definitively explain the origin of the symbol, although he claimed that he was introduced to the Enneagram symbol after visiting an Afghan monastery. His philosophy, however, can be observed in the modern Enneagram which its three intelligence centers.

Note that Ichazo himself denied that Gurdjieff's enneagrams were used as inspiration for his work. Nonetheless, Gurdjieff's philosophy on self-development were also presented in Enneagram form, albeit the points are different from the points promoted by Ichazo. We can safely say that it is Gurdjieff and Ichazo's use of the Enneagram which propelled its use in 21st century psychometry.

The Perennial Wisdom

You can call it Collective Consciousness. Or you can call it the universal truth. Perennial wisdom at its core refers to that which is true no matter who you are or where you are. The universal truth remains true no matter what your belief, culture, or religion is.

This could also mean different things for different kinds of people. For the spiritual, it's the one thread that connects us all. And make no mistake, there is something that connects us all.

The Human Experience is at the most basic level – the same thing. We all want self-actualization. We all want to do what we do best in order to be the best we can be. We find pleasure in achieving something that we feel is what we're here for. We all have a purpose. We all strive for success.

This cannot be denied. In fact, you can look back at one of the personality theories described in the previous chapter. Remember Maslow's hierarchy of needs. Look back at how we are exactly the same and tremendously different all at the same time.

All of us need water. All of us need food. We are all the same.

Some of us like to swim. Some of us like freshly cut grass. Some of us are the same.

You might be the only person who likes purple unicorns who also happen to love well-done steak and hate Metallica. Each one of us is unique.

It's in the details that we become completely utterly unique.

To some, success means being able to provide for a happy family. To some, it's climbing Kilimanjaro. To some, it's selling 1,000,000 records. To some, it's becoming president. To some it's about never needing anyone else. To some, it's the ability to not want anything at all.

We are all the same. Some of us are the same. Each of us is unique. We are all connected. This is a universal truth.

We are all driven by some restlessness. We always seem to be looking for something. There seems to be something missing, although we do not always know what it is. This is a universal truth.

We yearn to know who we are. We years to know why we are here. That is a universal truth.

It is so hard to look for the answers. And most of the time, we do not get the encouragement to look for answers. That is a universal truth.

However, if we keep searching beneath the surface to examine who we truly are and how different we are from each other, we might be surprised to know that despite such differences, we actually share a common humanity. That is a universal truth.

The Enneagram And The Interconnected Of Things

At the heart of the Enneagram system is the notion that there is an interconnectedness to things — that human beings don't just do things for no reason.

The reason may not be apparent at first glance, but it exists, and even before Freud posited the idea of the Id, the Ego, and the Superego, man had been thinking about this connectedness. This is evidenced in the way ancient Hindi philosophy espoused the notion of soul, self, and spirit, and the way the Ancient Greeks thought of man as a social and a reasoning being.

Our interconnectedness may not be apparent at first, but that's the expected result of a lack of introspection. To recognize the humanity of other people, we must first rise to the humanity of ourselves, and we can only do that by looking inward and self-inquiry. The enneagram helps us uncover the mystery that is ourselves. It is meant to accelerate integration especially during this modern era in which it is all too common for people to feel lost and fragmented.

The enneagram system does this by discerning our filters – that is, the way we view the world and consequently, our thinking processes, more clearly. It also shows us our core psychological issues by taking a look at what drives us and what we are most afraid of. From those insights, we could figure out our interpersonal strengths and weaknesses, as well the circumstances in which we shine and those that we might have difficulty with. All these are done through making use of personality patterns that you yourself have observed in yourself, and those that many wise men before us have used in decision-making. It's an invaluable tool that could change the way you see and live life.

In Modern Psychology, this common ground is presented in the form of the Big 5 theory

Many experts agree that there's something all human beings share – elements of personality that each of us have, albeit in varying degrees.

There are five, hence the name: (1) extraversion, (2) agreeableness, (3) openness, (4) conscientiousness, and (5) neuroticism. We'll run through them in order to gain better understanding of personality analysis, of which the Enneagram is a part.

As you go through the different sections for each Enneagram type, you would notice that many of the traits are directly or indirectly related to these five.

1. Extraversion – This refers to a person's social attitude. Those who are in the low end of the spectrum will not be outgoing and would prefer to be alone (what is generally described as introverted). Those on the high end of the spectrum will be the life of the party – they like being surrounded by other people. Sub-traits such as gregariousness and friendliness may be associated with this aspect.

2. Agreeableness – This aspect manifests in how a person shows kindness, warmness, and sympathy to other people.

Those on the high end of agreeableness have more empathy and are typically optimistic. They believe in harmony and cooperation above all. Those on the low end to be selfish and cynical and tend to feel that they're in competition with other people. Sub-traits associated with this aspect includes modesty and cooperativeness

3. Openness. This refers to a person's open-mindedness about everything. Those with a high degree of openness is the kind who enjoys trying new things. Those on the opposite side of the spectrum would rather stick to what they're used to. They're analytical but are resistant to change. Sub-traits for this personality aspect include imaginativeness, emotionality, liberalism, and adventurousness.

4. Conscientiousness. This refers to the degree at which an individual can control his impulses. Those on the high end of the spectrum tend to be quite self-disciplined.

Individuals with a high degree of conscientiousness tend to follow a plan and are usually regarded as workaholics whereas those with a low degree of conscientiousness tend to be impulsive. Sub-traits related to this aspect include orderliness, dutifulness, cautiousness, and reliability.

5. Neuroticism – This refers to a person's overall emotional stability. It's the ability to stay balanced even when in a difficult situation. Those who have high neuroticism tend to get upset easily and usually experience negative emotions. Those who are at the low end of the spectrum are able to think clearly even when faced with tough challenges. Sub-traits associated with this aspect include anxiety, depression, vulnerability, and depression.

An Ancient Solution To A Modern Problem

For some people, the enneagram is more than a psychometry technique. It can be used for spiritual awakening. This is rooted in Gurdjieff's philosophy -- that psychology and spirituality can both help in helping us understand our place in the universe and our reason for being.

It's a beautiful amalgamation of the Logic of psychology and the Wisdom of Spirituality. The enneagram was developed with the belief that psychometry knowledge is not wrong – just incomplete. This belief is shared by modern enneagram experts and the community as well. Mankind's knowledge of the universe is imperfect simply because the universe itself is so vast. One can even say that that is also a universal truth.

Many psychological and spiritual systems have been developed to address these insights including those that border on the mystical such as astrology, and the fantastical such as numerology, and those that have been developed by men of science, such as Freud and Carl Jung.

However, if the focus is growth, then one thing must always be taken into account – every human being is different. There are no boxes we should be put into. Growth can only occur if we're not limited to the box that we belong to.

What sets the enneagram apart is that it is in direct contradiction to what modern culture and education espouses – that we should all try to be the ideal version of a human being. However, going for this ideal version usually comes at a cost; it may cause us to deny who we are. That we have to discover, acknowledge, and embrace who we are is not as widely accepted as it should be. The enneagram does showcase how humans can transform themselves toward growth by nurturing certain aspects of their personality, but what it promotes above all is that the key is in ourselves.

We don't have to subscribe to some ideal that our mind has formulated without much thought about whether it's in keeping with who we are. We can simply be the best that we can be.

Beyond Our Personality Type

This is the splendid truth that the Enneagram system promotes – we are much more than our personality. It's true that we can use it to get started on the right path, and to recognize when we can use our strengths, and when our weaknesses could be our undoing, but it doesn't pigeonhole us to one thing.

Beyond our limitations as a fallible human being – and one with his own quirks, dreams, strengths, and weaknesses, there exists something divine in all of us. Whatever your religion may be, or even if you do not believe in a deity, within each of us is a divine spark – a higher purpose. Many of us, however, cannot feel this because we are no longer attuned to our true nature. Many of us are now so focused on surviving, and understandably so, that we feel we do not have the luxury to truly live.

Beyond out personality type, we have spirit. It is this spirit that keeps us waking up in the morning and drives you to do something. It's our essence. As we learn to become more aware of who we are and how the world affects us, and how our inner processes drive us to exhibiting certain behavior toward the world, we are able to get in touch with our essence. We can become more transparent. We can truly see, and feel, and understand. We can still walk the world the way we did, but with the growing realization of our connection to the entire human experience, and our higher purpose.

We are not just a bag of skin and bones walking the earth. We are spiritual beings who have our own personality. And when we stop trying to defend our personality and just recognize that it is just a part of us, we can be transformed. Our true nature can arise when we stop holding it back.

That's what the enneagram is designed for – to help us work on ourselves with the use of universal patterns and to reinforce self-observation and self-inquiry. That way, we can be truly integrated.

Chapter 5: Self-Awareness And The Enneagram

Use of the Enneagram can lead to self-awareness by uncovering the patterns of behavior that drive you and motivate you. It can help you better understand why you act the way that you do, leading you to take more responsibility for your own actions. When you better understand your dysfunctional behavior patterns and habits, you are better equipped to rise above them. The point of the Enneagram is to lead you as you explore it on a journey of self-discovery, increasing both your self-awareness and self-understanding. The Enneagram is meant to challenge you and to change you.

Everyone has their own unique strategies for protecting themselves. They depend on these "adaptive" strategies for their survival, and for dealing with unsolved trauma and unhealthy experiences. The skills and habits that you develop throughout your life are influenced in many ways by the circumstances and events that you experience during early childhood. These strategies become deeply rooted in your psyche as a child.

It is commonly understood that there are also some parts of your personality that you were simply born with. Exploring Enneagram can help you learn the difference between traits that you were born with and traits that you have acquired along the way. It can help you learn the difference between your personality and your character.

As an adult, you may over-identify with certain traits of your personality, and this can cause you to fall out of balance. When you rely too much on some parts of your personality, you end up building yourself up around those few parts. Your sense of self becomes associated with these limited personality traits, and you start to believe that this is who you really are. In actuality, there may be much more to you than you believe. You may not even recognize that you are not accessing all of your true self.

Enneagram exploration exposes your personality as a mask. Your mask is what keeps you trapped in the misconceptions of who you think you are. It protects you from the pain and the emotional wounds that you may have experienced in childhood. Enneagram teaches you how you have been mistakenly focusing too much on your false self, and shows you how to release your essential nature. It helps you learn the truth about yourself without any illusions.

You must be able to observe yourself before you can correct yourself. Enneagram can help you reclaim your essential self, with no layers, and no protection. It uncovers the real you and helps you integrate all different aspects of yourself. It aids you in understanding and accepting the fact that you are not always who you were meant to be. You have to understand this in order to remove your false self and to get to your true self.

Mapping out your personality with Enneagram can help you make sense of your feelings and reactions. It reveals to you how your habits have become your coping mechanisms, even if they are unhealthy. Enneagram helps you uncover the traps and patterns that may be keeping you from living your life to the fullest. It discloses the ways in which you may be relying on unconscious patterns and hanging on to self-defeating ways. Some of these habits may be holding you back from reaching your full potential.

Enneagram shows you your deep-rooted needs, fears, passions, and areas of growth. It points out your healthy and unhealthy patterns of behavior. Learning more about yourself can prevent you from becoming too rigid in your own responses and patterns, and from getting stuck in unhealthy habits. It can help you work through your own limitations and learn strategies to release them. Better understanding your type will help you make the most of your strengths, and help you to recognize and deal with your weaknesses. When you understand your automatic emotional responses fully, you are better equipped to handle the challenges that come your way.

Enneagram will allow you to see the good, the bad, and the ugly of your personality. Gaining this self-awareness can prevent you from continuing to practice the worse traits of your personality. It allows you to rewire your thoughts and behaviors, and to focus on further developing the healthier traits and characteristics that make up your personality.

When stressed, you may be even more likely to return to automatic tendencies of your personality type. You will be naturally inclined to follow your intuition, instead of exploring new options of reacting. Enneagram helps you understand how you approach the world.

It widens your perspective and makes you question whether you want to keep responding the way you have been responding. It lets you look back on your past behavior, recognize your patterns, and see how you have been holding yourself back. It lets you get to the root of your challenges quickly and shows you how to get unstuck. Enneagram can help you to set healthy boundaries for your time and energy, and better organize your existence. Going through this process encourages you to set goals for adjusting and developing your personality. It gives you a message that you may never have heard before and teaches you how to transform.

An additional benefit of discovering yourself through Enneagram is that this tool will teach you all about your strengths, special talents, and what makes you uniquely you. It will highlight how you can use these gifts to the best of your ability, and which parts of yourself may have some hidden strengths. Enneagram connects you with your best self. Going through this process can help you gain confidence, and increase your empathy and compassion for both self and others.

Digging into the Enneagram requires a lot of emotional energy. The good news is, even though learning about yourself may make you uncomfortable and thrown off balance, it also will make you curious to know more!

Spiritual Value of the Enneagram

Sacred Enneagram is not a religion or a spiritual philosophy; however, it is grounded in spiritual knowledge. The teachings of Enneagram contain a lot of sacred languages, and they respect all spiritual backgrounds and beliefs. The spirituality that is associated with Enneagram is not the same as biblical spirituality.

Enneagram is increasingly being used in counseling or therapy sessions that are faith-based. Many religious groups also incorporate Enneagram teachings into their practice and studies. It is a tool that allows its users to contemplate themselves deeply, and people who identify as being religious or spiritual are often drawn to this.

Enneagram is known in many circles to be a powerful tool of spiritual transformation. After all, it is meant to help you on a lifelong journey of discovery. Enneagram can help open you up to deeper levels of understanding and insight and can support you on your spiritual journey. Enneagram can help you grow in the ways you wish to grow. Many people just do not live up to their true potential and do not use the gifts that they have been given. They have lost connection with their God-given identity.

Many people believe that spirituality is about waking up to your personal illusions and becoming more human and more real. Enneagram helps you integrate your true identity with your false identity, and to become who you were really meant to be. It shows you both the good and the bad of your personality traits. Enneagram outlines the spiritual obstacles that may be getting in the way of your growth, according to your type. It helps you understand your patterns so that you can be better equipped to change them.

Exploring Enneagram leads you to see yourself and your world in a different way. It offers the opportunity for fresh spiritual perspectives. It helps you to figure out what habits and responses may be getting in the way of your path. It points out what is limiting you in your journey. It shows you the ways in which you lie to yourself and how you can get back to your true self. Enneagram points out what is getting in the way of gaining interpersonal and spiritual happiness. You can learn ways of responding that are not so automatically and will not be so limited in your spiritual relationship. Enneagram essentially shows you a path for developing your identity and spirituality based on your personality type.

The Enneagram is just one tool for spiritual transformation and should be explored in conjunction with other practices such as worship, communion, prayer, and the study of scripture. Self-observation, combined with whatever spiritual practices you follow can help you let go of negative reactions and help you become your best self. This combination can help you find your own distinct path to enlightenment. Self-awareness can most definitely lead to spiritual awareness.

Enneagram teachings show us that there are many different ways of being. In fact, there are nine distinct ways to nurture yourself. It is also said that there are nine unique contemplative prayer combinations that align with each Enneagram personality type. The truth is, all personality types could benefit from the message that they should stop trying to measure up, and instead focus on finding their true selves. Self-knowledge can take you to a very meaningful place.

Chapter 6: The Three Center

The Basis of Three

Earlier, we briefly mentioned the three main Centers of the Enneagram, those points of the inner equilateral triangle (9, 3, and 6), which give a central basis for defining the way each of the Enneatypes process. Essentially, we do have the overall division of the Enneatypes and how they process split into the three Center types, Heart (Feeling: 2, 3, and 4), Mind (Thinking: 5, 6, and 7), and Body (Instinctive, Gut: 1, 8, and 9). Additionally, within each of the Enneatypes, we have the same breakdown of processing, Heart, Mind, and Body.

Just because your primary way of processing events may be, say, Instinctive, it does not mean that you don't Think or have Feelings that align with how you process as well. It is only by examining all of the ways that we process events, good or bad, positively or negatively, that we can formulate where we are at in our evolution into a Higher Awareness.

Within each of the Center types, an individual will process things, both positively and negatively, based on their primary Center. For example, someone who is a 5, which falls under the Thinking Center, will have their greatest strengths and liabilities in how they process, respond, and do things from the standpoint of thinking. The same would be true of someone who was a 9, where their greatest assets and weaknesses would come from a place of instinctual behaviors.

When we get into the actual Enneatypes, we will delve even closer into how each of Centers processes things individually, as they can have some slight and some major differences. As we learn how to process these Centers, whether from a whole or more individualistic perspective, we cannot properly develop in our evolution of one Center, without having it affect the other two. For now, let's take a look at how these separations can affect us on a more general scale, according to the Enneagram model.

Heart

The drive of those who fall within the Heart Center is that of emotions, feelings. The Heart is the core of our being, that place of understanding. The Heart is aware of when things feel right or wrong to us. It is up to us to listen to that voice of feeling and emotion. Our Heart is our truth-teller. When things resonate with our Heart and feel right, our Heart will open up and connect us to the rest of the world. When it is feeling hurt, or not in synch because it senses something is not right, it closes itself off for protection, unwilling to go any further down the path of pain. How the Heart responds to events and the world around us, tells us of the quality of the life we are currently living.

For good or bad, the most commonly felt emotion of the Heart Center is shame. Transversely, the other side of the shame emotion is pride. Those with strong Heart Center connections have a strong need for validation, but don't always know how to give themselves that kind of self-love, and turn instead to others for validation and approval. The self-image of Heart-centered people is found through the eyes of others, for it is only then that they can try to understand who they are. The downside of this is that they will often give up the core of who they are in order to meet the approval and validation of others.

When Heart Center people don't find the attention that they inherently need through others, they tend toward the feelings of shame, but they also feel a deficiency in themselves, an emptiness of which they don't understand how to fill.

On the strength side, Heart Center people tend to be caring, helpful, and supportive people. They lean toward positive attitudes, exuberance, with strong creativity. Even with their strengths, however, they tend toward adopting these qualities in order to find approval in and through the other people around them.

Mind

The drive of those who fall within the Mind Center is that of thought and intelligence. The Mind is the core of our self, that place of wisdom. The Mind recognizes that we need a connection to the presence in the now, and believe that presence can be equated to intelligence. It is up to us to develop our sense of guidance and direction from within. Our Mind becomes that guide, as we analyze events, and take the wisdom of action and result from them. When it is confused because it perceives that something is not right, it reaches for a path of stillness, trying to connect to a place of better understanding through intelligence, which can generally be reached with a quieting of the Mind, coming to a grounded place from which to examine things from a mental stronghold.

For good or bad, the most commonly felt emotion of the Mind Center is fear. Transversely, the other side of the fear emotion is perception backed by courage and strategic thinking. Those with strong Mind Center connections have a strong need for remaining grounded. By maintaining a steady, grounded sense of self, they feel secure. Security is a paramount need for those with strong Mind Centers. They need to feel secure in their selves, their beliefs, and in their ability to strategize.

When Mind Center people can't find the essence of security that they inherently need, they tend toward the feelings of fear and panic, but they also tend to start isolating themselves from others and get lost in over thinking things, pushing them further away from connecting with others and the world around them.

On the strength side, Mind Center people tend to be courageous, loyal, considerate, and imaginative people. They lean toward strong self-reliance, dependability, and usually keep a calm head in times of crisis. Even with their strengths, however, it is all too easy for those with strong Mind Centers to isolate and disconnect from the rest of the world.

Body

The drive of those who fall within the Body Center is that of instinct and survival. The Body is the core of our physical existence, that place of being alive. The Body recognizes that we need a connection to our environment. It is up to us to develop our presence within our environment, and exert what control we can over it for our own survival and well-being. Our Body becomes that control, as we gain a sense of feeling alive as we protect ourselves and those around us. When the hackles on our neck rise up, we get that feeling of being gut-punched, or any other manner of physical reactions that signal danger to us because it perceives that something is not right, we tend to lose confidence and pull back from living a full existence.

For good or bad, the most commonly felt emotion of the Body Center is anger. Transversely, the other side of the anger emotion is determination and a feeling of protectiveness toward others. Those with strong Body Center connections have a strong need for remaining autonomous. Their anger is commonly directed at feelings of someone else messing with their sense of autonomy. They need to feel in control of themselves and their environment at all times.

When Body Center people can't find the essence of self and control that they inherently need, they tend toward the feelings of anger and stubbornness. They can become rigid and judgmental in their ways of thinking, as well as very dominating. They are afraid of showing any vulnerability, as their core concept is directly related to survival.

On the strength side, Mind Center people tend to be hard-working, dependable, conscientious people. They lean toward strong self-reliance, adaptability, and are very protective of those around them for whom they care. Even with their strengths, however, it is all too easy for those with strong Mind Centers to try and dominate and control the world around them, becoming quickly angered if that is not possible.

The Law of Three

The three Centers are a large part of who we are and how we react to ourselves, events, and the world around us. The primary Center, under which our Enneatype falls, is the Center which we are most comfortable with, and it dominates how we react to anything and everything. Our focus and attention are most guided by this Center, as a core nature of who we are, may be best understood as being "hard-wired" into our very nature.

We also have ties to one of the other three as a supporting role to our dominant trait. It generally becomes the second most developed in our nature. The third trait is also present within us all, although it will generally be the least developed, and can become an inherent blind spot when we are trying to move up our evolutionary ladder toward a higher state of awareness.

How these instincts are prioritized within our personal Enneagram largely dictates how we react to our world and ourselves and can teach us just what we may need to focus on in order to advance more quickly.

Chapter 7: The Helper

Type two personality is known as the helper and the giver. This personality type is one which focuses on helping others. Some of the primary words used to describe the helper are people-pleaser, demonstrative, possessive, and generous. The stress line for the helper shifts from a type two to a type eight, while the growth line shifts from a type two to a type four.

What is the Helper?

Stevie Wonder, Danny Glover, Martin Sheen, Elizabeth Taylor, and Richard Thomas (John boy Walton) are all considered to have a type two personality. People who have this personality type are typically warm and caring individuals. Not only are they generous but they are highly compassionate and don't tend to pass judgment. They are driven by their need to help others and can often be found in professions such as non-profits and volunteering at soup kitchens ("Type Two," n.d).

A type two's biggest desire is to be loved while their biggest fear is the feeling of being unwanted or unloved. In fact, one of the biggest reasons they focus on helping people is to fulfill this desire. They believe that the more they help people, the more people will enjoy their company and care about them. It is this feeling that makes helpers take so much time out of their day to make sure they are fulfilling their mission of helping other people.

People quickly see that type two personalities have big hearts. Therefore, they are drawn to helpers. Unfortunately, this can also cause problems because there are many people who are more interested in taking advantage of helpers. For many type two personalities, this becomes a problem because they don't often have the courage to defend themselves against people who take advantage of them. While some are able to defend themselves, many others continue to help people because they fear that people will not like them if they don't help..

Individuals with a type two personality are similar to a sponge. They tend to soak up emotions from other people, which can cause them to feel overwhelmed by all the different emotions. If they don't know how to release these emotions, they can be prone to emotional outbursts as this allows them to relieve the pressure. Because of this, it is important for them to find a balance between feeling loved by other people and loving themselves. No matter how much love you feel from someone else, it will never substitute self-love.

Levels of Integration

Healthy Level

A level one type two is the best level that you can reach. These types of people don't ever think that they should be rewarded for helping. People who reach this level are known to be selfless and help people because they feel true unconditional love for others, even those who have wronged them or others in the past. They believe that it is a privilege to be accepted by other people and be a part of their lives (Cloete, n.d.).

A level two type two is similar to a level one, however, these types sometimes believe that they should receive some help back. While they are extremely warm, compassionate, and caring individuals, they also hold more realistic expectations of how people can take advantage of them. However, they don't always act when they think they are being taken advantage of ("Type Two," n.d.).

A level three type two tends to take care of themselves as much as they take care of other people. They like to maintain a good balance, however, if it comes down to either help themselves or another person, they will help the other person first. Like the higher type two personalities, they are very nurturing, warm, caring, and generous. They believe that everyone has an ultimate good about them (Cloete, n.d.).

Average Level

A level four type two will have a lot of helpful qualities and good intentions. They don't often feel that they are entitled to help from other people. However, they also brag about how helpful they are. They believe that people should acknowledge their behavior and reward them. However, they don't often look for materialistic rewards, they would rather receive a reward through praise (Cloete, n.d.).

A level five type two personalities expect a return from the people they help. Those at a level five also tend to feel so strongly towards helping people that they can come off as more pushy than helpful (Cloete, n.d.). They don't fully understand the line between being helpful and becoming overly helpful.

A level six type two personality can also become overbearing when they are helping others (Cloete, n.d.). They believe that they do deserve rewards, however, they are not always open about this belief. They feel that they are irreplaceable and have a strong sense of self-importance.

Unhealthy Level

When a helper is at a level seven, they can often be manipulative. While they still like to help other people, they also feel more entitled to help (Cloete, n.d.). For example, if a type two personality helps you with raking your lawn, he or she will tell you how much you owe him or her the next time they need or want something. Unlike healthy level type two's, this unhealthy level will often think that he or she shouldn't complete any actions for free. In a sense, level seven type two's always want something back, a reward of sorts, for their helpful behavior.

A level eight type two is similar to a level seven but often feels entitled to any type of favor they want from someone else (Cloete, n.d.). These favors can come in the form of money, house work, or sexual activities. Someone who ranks at level eight for a type two personality is generally not shy about asking what they want. Furthermore, they don't possess the warm and caring personality that the majority of type two personalities do when they are asking for help.

A level nine type two is the lowest level that a type two personality can have. Similar to the other unhealthy levels, they feel highly entitled to favors and jobs performed by other people (Cloete, n.d.). However, they will also justify their behavior and the way they treat people because of the helpful nature of their personality. They believe that because they treat people with kindness, they are able to act towards a person how they wish.

Subtypes of the Helper

Social Category is Ambition

Type two personalities have a lot of ambition and can often be seen taking on leadership roles. They like to feel like they are important and needed, therefore, they will find people and organizations who need them. Because of their caring and helpful personality, people are quickly attracted to them, which easily helps them engage groups of people. This can also allow the helper to get what they want out of the groups, such as completing tasks or getting more help from others (Cloete, n.d.).

However, type two personalities often feel uncomfortable when they are alone. This happens for several reasons, one being that they feel they are not doing whatever they can to help someone. Therefore, many professionals agree that helpers will use their personality in order to block out their uncomfortable feelings. The busier they are, the less likely they will be able to feel what they don't want to feel (Cloete, n.d.).

Self-Preservation Category is Privilege

This is the countertype of type two. In fact, they are often mistaken to be a type seven personality. A type two can often cause other personalities to feel like they need to be protected because of their helpful nature. Because of this, type two is often considered to be a little child-like and shy. They don't mind feeling like they are being protected, however, they also don't want to become too dependent on someone else. They feel that their sense of self-protection is a privilege, so they treat it with care. Furthermore, they have a big fear of rejection, which makes them feel like they have to protect themselves more than someone else would (Cloete, n.d.).

One-on-One Category is Seduction

Type two personalities are very giving, compassionate, and thought to be extremely selfless, however, this doesn't mean that they don't want to feel important to someone. No matter what level a type two personality is, whether healthy, average, or unhealthy, they still feel a need to receive compassion and love from someone. Therefore, when type two personalities get into an intimate relationship, they start to feel this connection very strongly. They will often use the caring and loving parts of their personality towards their partner so they can feel these emotions back.

Once the type two personality gets into a very close relationship, they can start to feel very passionate. Of course, this passion comes with positives and negatives. For example, one positive is they will begin to feel more comfortable and trust their partner. However, one negative is they will start to have trouble taking no for an answer. In fact, they might find it hard to set and follow limits (Cloete, n.d.).

Relationships with Other Types

Type two personalities tend to get along with type one and type three the best because these personalities are type two's wings. However, they also get along with generally any type of personality. But, of course, they will struggle with some personalities more than others. For example, type two and type five struggle with getting along. While they will eventually get along, type two views type five as a challenging personality that is often difficult to form a relationship with ("Relationships (Type Combinations)," n.d.).

Some of these types are better off as friends and co-workers rather than to be in a romantic relationship. For example, type four and type two get along exceptionally well and often create a very warm and compassionate relationship. However, they make better friends than romantic partners.

Wing Types

The two wings for type two personality are type one and type three. Both of these wings not only help type two to manage their personality better, but also involves challenges. When it comes to positives, the type one will bring more balance to the type two by having them help everyone and not their favorite people. Furthermore, type one helps them establish boundaries so people don't consistently take the type two for granted. Type one can also help type two improve their environment. When it comes to challenges, type one can make type two have unrealistic expectations, become too hard on themselves for mistakes, become sensitive to criticism, and cause them to neglect themselves (Cloete, n.d.).

The type three personality can provide type two advantages by helping them with their focus, self-esteem, and the ability to adapt to other people and their surroundings. The challenges that type two faces with a type three wing is the act of neglecting themselves because they become too focused on their work and become selective when it comes to helping people (Cloete, n.d.).

Center Point

If you have a type two personality, you will sit under the heart center point and externalize your feelings of shame (Cloete, n.d.). This is often what makes you become the best person you can be, which is why you are often seen as helpful and supportive. In a sense, you use your shame in order to create a better person and help others. This provides you with an image of yourself as being needed and well-liked, which makes you feel better about your shame.

Type two's strengths:
- **Helpful**
- **Generous**
- **Supportive**
- **Caring**
- Relationships
- **Sensitive**

Type two's weaknesses:
- Dependent
- **Demanding**

- **Prideful**
- **Privileged**
- **Intrusive**

How to Grow Personally

Remember to Ask People What They Need

A type two personality wants to help people in any way possible. Because of this, they often forget to ask the person what type of help they really need or want. Sometimes people don't want to receive the help you are giving them, which means you aren't really helping them at all. It is important for other people, and yourself, to make sure that you are using your energy on the people who really want the help. Don't be afraid to ask them if you can help them in any way. If people really need the help, they will let you know. If they tell you that they don't need your help, just let them know that you are available if they ever do. Often, when people know that you are available to help them is all they need to hear to feel loved and cared about (Cloete, n.d.).

Be Conscious of Your Motives

As stated above, there are a few levels of type two personalities that expect certain things in return and start to feel entitled to being treated well because of the way they treat others. This is an example of poor interior motives, which is something that you should improve on if you begin to feel this way. While everyone has the internal feeling of wanting to receive some of the help and compassion they give to others, when you start to feel like you deserve this compassion and love because of your actions, you should take a step back and rethink your motives. You want to help other people because it's a part of your personality. You want to be compassionate to others because you hold a special personality that strongly advocates compassion. You want to use these important pieces of your personality to strengthen the lives of others and not cause harm (Cloete, n.d.).

Don't Forget About Yourself

You might think that you deserve rewards because you are forgetting to take care of yourself. This is often a weakness for someone with a type two personality. No matter what personality you have, it is important to make sure that you take time for yourself and give yourself the care you need, so you can live a happy and healthy life. Type two personalities often forget to take care of themselves because they are so fixated on taking care of other people. However, this can harm you in the end. Therefore, it is important to make sure to give yourself some care and pampering time just as you would for anyone else. Doing so will allow you to spread your unconditional love to others easier (Cloete, n.d.).

Chapter 8: Multidimensional Personality

The structure of the conventional Enneagram diagram is intended to help you visually, mentally and emotionally connect with the tool, showing you how the interrelation among the personality types works. Before we start dissecting it, I bet you're wondering why the system is numerically numbered 1-9. I was curious about it too. Does a higher numerical ranking imply that one personality type possesses more value?

Not at all! There's no difference in value between the larger and the smaller number. So just because someone is an Eight does not signify they are better than a Three.

The quickest way to understand the diagram is by starting from the outside layers and work your way in. Imagine drawing a circle. Then a triangle within the circle and let it touch all three corners.

Mark the three points of the triangle 9, 3 and 6 in clockwise position with 9 sitting at the top of the circle.

All you have to do now is make six equidistant points from the circumference of the circle and designate the remaining numbers 1,2,4,5,7,8 to fill in the gaps. Be sure to do it symmetrically and in a clockwise motion. Each of these numbers represents one of the primary nine personality types. If you're doing this activity by hand, you will begin to notice that the nine points can be connected in some way by inner lines and that points 3, 6 and 9 actually form an equilateral triangle. The remaining six points can be connected as shown in the diagram below. The importance of these inner lines leads us to another vital lesson when it comes to an understanding of the Enneagram of Personality tool.

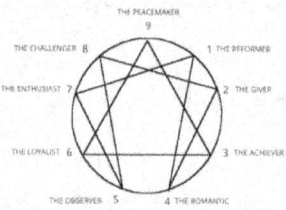

At a fundamental level, the tool is used to help a person identify their most dominant type within the nine-point system. However, there's more to it than meets the eye for those who want to dive deeper. There's also interconnectedness between the nine points. So, while you may find your basic personality to be a 2, it isn't uncommon to discover a little more of yourself in all nine types. This is where the Centers and Wings come into play.

As infants, we don't really have a developed sense of self. The ego has not yet been activated and if you're unclear about this, just spend some time in a park. Notice how the tiny infant in a pram has no sense of identity. He or she can barely tell the difference between their toes and fingers or whether a doll belongs to them or not. Then observe toddlers who are starting to become a little more self-aware. They can identify their parents and siblings but still don't have a sense of self. Then we have the five-year-olds playing together, chasing a ball around. The owner of the ball knows it belongs to him/her and he/she would probably cry if you grab it from him/her, but the self is still very fluid. Once they get to age seven and above, the self is well defined, and everything is about taking ownership and determining "me" and "mine." As children, we were not different. Depending on our environment, what our caregivers taught us, how they treated us and what we got exposed to, we developed a sense of self to help us fit into this world and survive.

We may, therefore, generalize that our formative years and all we were exposed to helped shape our personalities. We learned to depend more heavily on the personality type that would enable us to survive and feel safe in the world around us. Some of what we ended up choosing may be wonderful, but perhaps some aspects are not healthy at all, yet we still show up in the world as that person. Furthermore, it might be that we've neglected to develop and leverage the influences of the connected qualities and special abilities we may possess. That's why getting to know what center you belong to and what wings you're in possession of can be worthwhile. Let us further discuss the role of the three centers and the wings before jumping into each of the nine points in the next section.

The Centers:

These are centers of intelligence into which each of the numbered points will fall. Each center will contain three personality types. The triad consists of the thinking center, the feeling center, and the gut center.

Also known as the head, heart and gut centers respectively, these centers are designed and designated to the specific areas on the diagram intentionally. The centers are usually differentiated from each other based on how the person usually interprets life and others.

The Thinking Center:

The head types are usually too stuck in their head. They tend to withdraw from relationships. The head center is a cognitive center and the people in this triad love to think, analyze, and approach things with caution. Picture for a moment that you were at a party. If you're part of the thinking center, then your natural tendency and preference would be standing at or close to the door so you can have a better view and merely observe others.

Some authors like to refer to them as mental-based types. Their dominant emotion to keep in check is Fear.

The Feeling Center:

The heart types are usually people who engage in relationships and continuously seek out others. They are very concerned with feelings and their interactions with other people. Go back to that party scene again. This time instead of standing by the door to see who is present and what's happening around you, you'd be the first to mingle, introduce yourself to people and try to connect with as many people as possible.

Some authors will refer to these types as feeling-based types. Their dominant emotion to keep in check is Shame.

The Instinctive Center:

The gut types are instinctual. They are very direct and aren't afraid to be confrontational. People in this triad tend to act first and think and feel later. If we take that party example one last time, you'd know if this triad is your perfect fit by your approach from the moment you entered the room. Are you bold, loud, hearty and jovial in your interaction with others? Perhaps you come off too strong which others often find offensive or intimidating. And if you're the type of person who isn't shy when it comes to offering constructive criticism even if it is to the host of the party, then I'd say, this is your center of intelligence.

So, in other words, you have a specific unconscious emotional response that often surfaces as a result of the loss of contact between the everyday little self and the true self. The three centers, having been grouped into Thinking, Instinctive and Feeling centers, have as their dominant emotions Fear, Anger, and Shame respectively.

So, if you take the Enneagram test and discover you're a Type Six and after a little reflection it dawns on you that fear is definitely one of the biggest paralyzers holding you back from greatness, then you've just confirmed that you're dominantly in the Thinking Center.

The more disconnected you are from your true self, the tighter the grip of fear will be because that's the dominant unconscious emotion.

Each center of intelligence has certain liabilities and assets that are included in it which the assigned personality types that come under that group will possess. For example, Type Three falls into the "feeling center." This suggests their most dominant unconscious emotion to watch out for is Shame. It also means there are certain strengths and qualities they would possess in relation to "feelings" which is why they fall into that triad.

Just so we're clear, this doesn't mean you won't experience other emotions. Think of the group you're in as containing a theme.

Whatever your theme is, that will be your most dominant emotion to deal with.

The Wings:

The reason I believe wings are a significant aspect to include in your interpretation of your Enneagram results is that in truth, none of us can be entirely summed up by a single personality type.

We are unique and complex individuals, ever-evolving and changing from one moment to the next which means our character must also be a combination of various qualities. The wings help to integrate this concept into the system.

Although some teachers of the Enneagram argue that we only have one wing, even if we judge it from a strictly numerical point of view, the number 1 is connected to 2 on one side and 9 on the other. The type adjacent to the 1 is what we refer to as your wing. Just as a bird or plane needs both wings to fly, you need wings to soar. These wings are supposed to compliment your core personality. They connect you to your "closest neighbors" giving you access to different resources and characteristics that can be quite useful.

Are both wings equally dominant and do you need to develop each one individually?

I think the most important thing to recall when it comes to your wings is that you will resonate more with one side and that's okay. As years go by, that might change too, and you may find yourself switching and exhibiting more qualities of the wing that's less influential. Either way, it's good to become aware of both and figure out which one aligns best with your basic personality and the human being you want to become.

An effective way of approaching and understanding your wings:

As you lean more into your wings to one side or the other, you will expand your perspective and increase your capacity to deal with tension creating a bigger potential to reframe influencers that no longer serve you. Each core personality type comes with a connected "close neighbor" on each side of the nine-point system.

Chapter 9: Type One - The Perfectionist

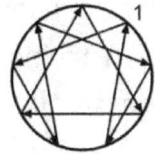

Dominant Traits
- **Self-controlled**
- **Purposeful**
- **Perfectionist**
- Principled

General Behavior

One of the defining characteristics of Ones is that they have a strong sense of ethical direction and conscientiousness. What does this mean? This is an individual who has a strong sense of good and bad with a perception which is clearly black or white. They have little time for the middle ground.

These strong ethical convictions make Ones very good at advocacy, and at championing campaigns or crusades, and they are very good teachers. They are driven by the desire to make the world a better place, and because of this, they will not shy away from trying to improve the world in even the smallest of ways. Even the smallest action makes a big difference in the end.

There is a caveat to interacting with Ones though, as mistakes are their kryptonite. A mistake is very unsettling for such a person. It is difficult to be perfect, so a mistake is often seen as a step in the wrong direction, a defect. Ones set standards too high for themselves, and many people cannot compare.

Furthermore, they also have a unique desire for order and organization.

Because of this, life is not always a walk in the park. Ones also struggle with disappointment from other people. The perfectionist in them makes them believe they are good; in fact, that they are the best. Because they place themselves on such a high pedestal, they tend to be impatient and wish for immediate results. This is perhaps out of the fear that waiting creates room for error.

Other than impatience, Ones also do not handle resentment well. They are strongly motivated by the desire to be the best, be the most right, to achieve greater things in life. This means that they don't have any room for resentment. Resentment to them is a sign of displeasure. If you live your life constantly working hard to be beyond reproach, the notion that someone is displeased or dissatisfied with your actions can be unacceptable.

Everyone deserves some criticism from time to time. Criticism helps you take a step back and review your actions, correct your mistakes, and come back stronger. However, this does not apply for Ones. In their minds, they are the best, and it is highly disappointing if they are criticized.

Typical Action Patterns

Perfectionists have some really good strengths. These are individuals who are very disciplined, so it is almost impossible to find them breaking the law. In school, they will be among the best students according to their teachers. They do everything right, they follow the rules, and they try to encourage other students to do the same. In the workplace, Ones are some of the best employees. They believe in showing up, doing their work, and earning their keep. They respect the workplace, the code of conduct, and do everything an employer would expect of an excellent employee.

From the moment they walk into an organization, the first thing they do is seek the rules and regulations. This is because of their principles. These are individuals whose lives are built around the principle that to interact with them and be in their good graces, you must also be doing the right thing. It takes a lot to make them go against their beliefs when it comes to following the rules.

Given their desire to pursue discipline, control, and morally upright life, perfectionists are often quite religious people. This is because religion is typically generally about the do's and don'ts. Whichever religion you follow, there are always set rules and regulations, and in many cases, there are punishments for contravening them. Religion gives life structure.

Perfectionism goes hand-in-hand with structure. This is why they appreciate rules. To engage perfectionists in a contract, an agreement, or anything else that might impose a systematic way of doing things on their lives, you must first put it in writing. A written agreement is not easy to backtrack on. This assures the Ones that they are doing their part, and that you are contract-bound to do your part too.

Ones prefer to take their time to analyze a situation before they act on it. This enables them to make sure everything checks out. They are meticulous in their analysis and leave no room for error. While this tends to be a good thing, the problem arises when they focus too much on something that everyone else feels is unnecessary. Their idea of perfection and living a life beyond reproach might make them focus a lot of their energy on something that is undeserving of all the time allocated to it. It gets even worse when they are required to act fast on an urgent matter.

Typical Thinking Patterns

Perfectionists have very strong convictions, and their belief in right and wrong makes them very strict about everything in life. This does not just apply to people around them, as it also applies especially to themselves. They worry about the perception other people have of them, as they have to be seen as the most morally upright individuals around. They believe themselves to be a beacon of hope for humanity. To effect change, they believe that you have to start by changing yourself.

They believe that they need to be good enough to warrant justification in their own eyes before they expect society to appreciate them for their goodness. While there is nothing wrong with trying to be the best, the way they go about it can be catastrophic. To be the best, some people try to create and assume an amazing persona that people can relate to. In the case of Ones, however, they will often end up doing something insane.

They also believe that overcoming adversity is the best way to prove to everyone else that they are perfect. It is not uncommon to find them engaging in acts that might be considered self-torture. They feel that they have a bigger purpose in life: the pursuit of the greater good. This is one type of person you might struggle to impress because they can't even trust themselves to have done the best.

Of course, there is nothing wrong with holding yourself in high regard. However, this comes at a cost for perfectionists. They don't just set very high standards for themselves; they keep pushing the standards higher. This desire to overachieve is too intense that they become unforgiving, not just with themselves, but with everyone else as well.

When engaging with a perfectionist, you will realize that most of their conversations are laced with statements concerning what should or should not be done. This might sound rather imposing on their audience, but this is just the way they are. Deep down, they have an inner critic that guides their entire idea of life and tells them what they must do to be seen as a good person. They follow the rules without question, as they believe this is what a good person should.

It is not uncommon for perfectionists to detach from affiliations when they feel they are no longer satisfactory. Their desire is for interactions that allow them room to portray the ideal picture of a good person. They believe that you should live your life according to the way they live theirs. After all, society has no better mirror around than them.

Typical Feeling Patterns

Relationships with perfectionists have a very high likelihood of strain and being unhealthy, especially if they are with someone who does not feel the same way about some things in their lives. Ones are not just 'uptight' about their ethical conduct: it is more of an obsession, which can turn into an unhealthy one at times. Everything in their lives is about rules where there is no room for fluidity. This is a neurotic problem which makes life difficult for anyone who believes in the alternative.

Because of this predisposition, perfectionists often come off as judgmental even when they don't mean it. It is in their nature to criticize people who go against the basic convention of right and wrong. They struggle to understand why everyone else struggles see things the way they do, something which ends up breeding resentment.

In a large group of friends, they will often come off as the sensitive one, because their go-to move in any situation is to follow the rules, even when people are excited about breaking the rules or pushing their limits. Trying to explain your way out of a predicament with a perfectionist is a waste of time. In their minds, you had to choose between good or bad, and you made your choice. It, therefore, follows that you must also accept the consequences. Ones believe that the consequences will remind you that you should do the right thing next time. After all, it is the law, right?

However, things don't always go according to plan, and this is the problem with living life on the extreme ends of decisions. Life is not about absolutes and should make room for errors. Unfortunately, perfectionists push their limits to a point where they end up unintentionally making the same mistakes they warn people against. Take the example of a perfectionist who believes that it is wrong to break the law. They feel so strongly about following the law that they may feel so irritated by someone who is intentionally breaking the law and end up breaking the law themselves in a bid to stop the other person from breaking the law. This, of course, is an extreme example. Perfectionists are very morally upright and will always try their best to make sure their lives are free of conflict, especially with the law.

How to Improve Your Life

Being a growth-oriented individual, there is probably a lot going on in your life at any given time. How you manage this will determine whether you endure stress or development healthily. You must learn to take care of yourself by allowing yourself sufficient time to relax and unwind and resisting the temptation to do everything yourself. Where possible, reach out to others to help you get some work done. Embrace teamwork and cooperate with those who agree to work with you so that you can foster healthy relationships.

Understand that people will not always see or do things the way that you expect them to. This is one of the issues that will trigger your aggression and anger from time to time. Some people will never follow instructions, perhaps because they don't understand them, or maybe because it is just their nature to be rebellious.

Do not hold back from experiencing your feelings. You might feel vulnerable when you are expressing them, but this is normal. Get in touch with your emotions. At times it may feel like your imperfections are obvious to everyone around you, but everyone else is dealing with their own imperfections too. Do not allow your insecurities about your emotions to take over your life, or hinder you from enjoying the goodness that lies within.

Try to manage your expectations in your interactions with other people. You might be very good at coaching people, and your instructions will also be very clear. However, people learn at different speeds. You will have to be patient with them so that they understand what you teach them. Remember that some lessons take longer to learn than others, so give them time to grasp your concept.

When people wrong you, do not take it too personally. This will irritate you and make your life a living hell. Let them own up to their mistakes and make amends for them.

Chapter 10: The Many Directions Of The Enneagram

You may have noticed by now that the numbers and symbols within the Enneagram are actually connected by lines. The only two numbers that are not connected by a line are 5 and 4. These lines indicate the direction in which a certain basic personality type could change. Sometimes this change is for the better, while other times it is definitely for the worse, and in some cases it can even be extreme.

There are two basic directions of the Enneagram: the **Direction of Disintegration (Stress)** and the **Direction of Integration (Growth)**. They are both denoted by a sequence of numbers which will always follow each other in either one direction or the other. Depending on the direction in which the numbers are going, the individual is either heading towards a healthier mental state or an unhealthier mental state.

In the case of **stress**, the sequence of numbers is 1-4-2-8-5-7-1. This means that where your current personality state is at, it will eventually move towards the next number in line – no matter what that number might be. So for example, if your current personality is a two, your next personality trait will resemble that of an eight. These changes are inevitable fi they are not controlled, because one number naturally moves towards another in the order of the Enneagram. The more time you spend in this enchantment of personalities, the worse the situation will become for you. Likewise, you will notice that there is no clear end for this distinction. The personality spiral could actually continue on indefinitely if it is not stopped at some point. So for example, if you start at one and reach seven, you would then go back to one and continue the process all over again but this time in an even more difficult mental state.

In the case of **growth**, the same numbers apply but in the opposite order. They are 1-7-5-8-2-4-1. As its name suggests, growth is the positive version of this direction in the sense that the person is becoming better as they follow this order of numbers. The more the individual is able to follow this pattern, the more likely they will be to live a happier and more fulfilling life. However, this does not mean that this order is permanent either. If something were to go wrong in the process and the person starts moving towards a more negative mental state, they will in fact retract back to the previous number and the situation will quickly become worse.

All human beings experience each direction of growth and stress at various points in their lives. No one is just stable at a single number without ever flinching. However, the purpose of the Enneagram is to help show you where you will end up in the future if you do not take any action in your life. You need to constantly be aware of where you are finding yourself at the moment, so that you can properly react to any new situation or development as soon as it happens. This will allow you to determine your future more easily and to make realistic plans and expectations of everything that you can achieve. Perhaps even more importantly, a good understanding of the Enneagram will also help you to bring valuable advice to other people and to make sure that you stop them from making a bad decision before it is too late. Understanding this style of the human psyche is beneficial on a number of different levels, not just that of the individual.

The Instincts Behind the Enneagram

We can now shift our focus on the inherent instincts that make up the psychology of any individual. You can consider these instincts the third level of the Enneagram symbol, although they may not be visually present in it.

Our instincts are something that we are born with, and interestingly, we all have the same ones. They will of course differ in their strength from one individual to another, but the basic point is that they will always be present within us and they will always mark a reaction to everything that we do in life.

The three inherent instincts for all human beings are as follows:

The self-reservation instinct – this is one of our most important instincts because it ensures that we always find a way to remain safe and to keep our loved one safe as well. This is the instinct that helps us deal with danger and also the ones that gives us a quick overview of how we would fair in confrontation with another living thing. This is not just the case when it comes to measuring up our strength against another human being, but also against perhaps an animals or a dangerous place in nature. For example, if you were placed in front of a lion, your instinct would be to somehow find a way to run away from the lion and not be eaten. Your inherent instinct would not be to fight the lion! This is a crucial point in our psychology and it is the instinct that has helped us survive for generations and thousands of years. Those who undermine the importance of this instinct will inevitably end up dead or seriously injured. Although some of the other instincts may perhaps have more varieties to them, this is one instinct that you should really make it a point to listen to all the time.

The sexual instinct – the second instinct is one that is crucial for the survival of our species. It is an instinct that helps us to remember who we are and what our purpose is in the world. However, it is not just based on a primary need for sexual attraction, but instead for love overall. We are not creatures that can cope to be on our own. We need a certain amount of love and attraction if we are to truly feel fulfilled and one with the world that surrounds us. As technology has developed in our world, this instinct has actually become less and less prominent because people are not feeling the connection with one another that they were once able to. It is unclear how this issue will develop in the future, but the important thing is to not forget that this instinct does exist within us.

The social instinct – this is our third and final universal instinct that has a profound impact on our personalities. We are social beings, and we need the help of other humans in order to feel like we are part of something important and something that will bring us joy and happiness in the future. Some people have tried to disregard this instinct as anything at all important, but in doing so they have managed to make themselves feel miserable and abandoned because we cannot go on for long without the comfort of society. Certainly, this doesn't mean that any company is better than no company, but in many cases, we have tried to set the pedestal for people to please us too high up instead of just enjoying the joy that people can bring us.

The interesting thing about these instincts is that, much like our personalities, these instincts are also strong at different levels among different people. We do not all possess an equal level of each, and we never will. The important thing is to learn how to balance between them and how to find the right spot where you are making the most of each instinct and allowing it to have a positive contribution to your life. People who stray too far away from their instincts will soon find that life becomes unbalanced and their personalities begin to shift along the lines of the Enneagram.

Regardless, one of these instincts will always be dominant in an individual and it will cause them to lean more towards one type of personality rather than another. You cannot force yourself to be strong in a particular instinct, you can only use the one that you were born with as the dominant one. As you move through life and you experience both positive and negative things, you will notice that these instincts will guide you towards the path that fits you level of instincts and also your own personality. Remember that even though people often describe our instincts as having our best intentions in mind and helping us survive, the truth is that they are quite general in their understanding of life. What your instinct tells you to do may not always be the right thing to do if your personality is not properly aligned on the levels of the Enneagram. For example, there will be times when your instincts try to make you do things just because they feel good and not because someone else will be able to benefit from them. This is quite the dangerous predicament to be in, because it means that you will behave in ways that are negative both for yourself and for your environment. In order to prevent such things from happening, you need to ensure that you regularly check your psychological position on the Enneagram, so that you can quickly react to a negative situation if one such situation does occur. Keep as many elements of your psyche in mind as often as possible, because this is the only way to both create and maintain the balance that you need to live a happy life.

Chapter 11: The Three Center

The Basis of Three

Essentially, we do have the overall division of the Enneatypes and how they process split into the three Center types, Heart (Feeling: 2, 3, and 4), Mind (Thinking: 5, 6, and 7), and Body (Instinctive, Gut: 1, 8, and 9). Additionally, within each of the Enneatypes, we have the same breakdown of processing, Heart, Mind, and Body.

Just because your primary way of processing events may be, say, Instinctive, it does not mean that you don't Think or have Feelings that align with how you process as well. It is only by examining all of the ways that we process events, good or bad, positively or negatively, that we can formulate where we are at in our evolution into a Higher Awareness.

Within each of the Center types, an individual will process things, both positively and negatively, based on their primary Center. For example, someone who is a 5, which falls under the Thinking Center, will have their greatest strengths and liabilities in how they process, respond, and do things from the standpoint of thinking. The same would be true of someone who was a 9, where their greatest assets and weaknesses would come from a place of instinctual behaviors.

When we get into the actual Enneatypes, we will delve even closer into how each of Centers processes things individually, as they can have some slight and some major differences. As we learn how to process these Centers, whether from a whole or more individualistic perspective, we cannot properly develop in our evolution of one Center, without having it affect the other two. For now, let's take a look at how these separations can affect us on a more general scale, according to the Enneagram model.

The Law of Three

An enneagram is considered a 3 x 3 arrangement of all nine personality types we have seen in the figure represented in chapter one above in three centers. These centers are; the instinctive center, the feeling center, and the thinking center. Each of these three centers has three personality types, hence a 3 x 3 arrangement.

For instance, personality type 9 has its unique strengths and weaknesses involving its instincts. It's the reason why it is in the Instinctive Center. Similarly, type 6 has its unique assets and liabilities in its thinking and hence falls within the Thinking center, and so on.

The fact that each type is within a center is not an arbitrary occurrence. It merely means that every single kind emanates from a peculiar interaction with a cluster of features that classify that particular center. These features often revolve around an expansively unconscious emotional response with the loss of contact at the core oneself.

Each one of the centers possesses different emotions that contribute to defining each personality type. The instinctive center, the feeling is anger and rage, the characteristic of the feeling center is the shame, and finally, the thinking center characterized by fear.

You may be thinking 'does it mean that if I have one emotion, I cannot have the other?' Well, No! Everyone experiences all these three emotions; anger, shame, and fear. However, in each of these centers, the personality of the type is adversely affected by that center's particular emotional theme.

Because each center has its emotion that influences its character/personality, each one of them has a particular way to cope with its dominant feeling. Let us briefly see how each personality type responds to their dominant emotions.

The Instinctive center

- This center is composed of personality types 1,8 and 9. Personality type 8 often acts out of anger and their inherent energy. Meaning that, when they feel anger building up within them, they respond to it immediately by physically raising their voice or fighting forcefully. It is evident that this personality type allows their rage to get the best of them by expressing it physically. They are merely said to be violent.

- Personality type 9 often deny their anger and mechanical energy so that they do not portray their true self. They often hide behind the phrase 'I'm not a person that gets angry.' They are often out of touch with their anger as they feel that their violence threatens them. In other words, they get angry as anyone could. However, the bright side is that they try as much as they can to stay away from their anger and darker side by focusing on their relationships and its interaction with the rest of the world.

Personality type 1 often try as much as they can to control or repress their anger and instinctual energies. They strongly feel the need to take charge of their emotional feelings especially anger. They hide their hatred behind their superego, which is often the foundation of their social structures and defines the manner in which they interact with others.

The Feelings center

This center is comprised of personality types 2, 3 and 4. Personality types two often control their shame by trying hard to lire others into liking them and perceiving them as good people. They often find the need to convince themselves that they are good people. In other words, they force themselves to try and show love to people despite their negative feelings of resentment and dislike towards the person. For them, it's easy to show people their positive emotions as long as they are liked in return, hence controlling their feelings of shame.

Personality type 3's often denies their shame. They do not let their emotional feelings of -shame to get the best of them despite their underlying inadequacies. For them, trying to become more valuable and successful is the best way to cope with their shame. Hence, they try hard to perform well so that they can be accepted. Often, they work extra hard to attain success so that they self-distract from feelings of shame and fear of failure.

Finally, type 4's tries to control their shame by paying attention to their uniqueness and the things that make them unique. These things include their talents, personal features/traits as well as feelings. They highlight their creative nature as a way of handling their shameful feelings, although they are vulnerable to feelings of inadequacy. in other words, bury their heads in a world of fantasy and romance so that they do not have to face the things affecting them most in their lives.

The Thinking Center

This center comprises personality types 5, 6 and 7. Personality type 5 often expresses fear about the outer world as well as their capacity to cope with fear. In other words, they often withdraw from the rest of the world around them as a way to deal with their anxiety. They are secretive and isolated and prefer when they are left alone so that they can use their minds to interact with nature. As they begin to understand their self, they rejoin the world and participate in different activities with people. However, in spite of their efforts, they often do not feel confident enough to participate fully.

Personality type 6 exhibits the most fear of all three personality types within this center. They portray anxiety that causes them to feel out of touch from their knowledge and confidence. Unlike example 5, this personality cannot trust their minds and hence, try hard to find something outside that can reassure them. This includes such things as philosophies, authorities, income, relationships, values, and beliefs among others. However, despite the many structures that they put up, they cannot seem to overcome their self-doubt and anxiety.

Personality type 7 have a fear of their inner world. Most strive hard to stay away from feelings of anxiety, loss, pain, and deprivation. For them to cope with these feelings, they occupy their minds on exciting possibilities and opportunities given. In other words, they try to pursue one option after another just so that they distract themselves from fear.

Chapter 12: Identifying Your Enneagram Type

With what you have learned from the book, you probably have some idea of which type you are. Some people do immediately determine their type. However, it can be a lengthy and frustrating process for others. It takes a lot of discussion, exploration, introspection, and self-observation. You might even find out something about yourself that you dislike.

Identifying Your Personality Type On Your Own

There is one thing to remember when typing yourself and others – there really is no grand secret to it. You simply have to know about the traits that go with each type as well as the behaviors that result from such traits.

Make no mistake, analysis takes a lot of nuance because there are so many quirks to each personality type, and human beings are complex and layered.

Avoid focusing too much on one trait. Note that one trait could appear in different types. However, how people manifest those traits could differ. For example, empathy in a Helper is brought by the need to love and be loved, whereas a Peacemaker being considerate is brought by the need to maintain harmony. Here is another example: Reformers tend to defy the rules because they want something better. Challengers tend to defy the rules because they do not respect rules. Try to see each type in its entirety – including fears and desires. In addition, teach all you can about the other types, especially those that are traditional wings to what you deem to be your basic type.

Converse with people and reach out to the Enneagram community. We have so much to learn from other people. We all share the human experience at a certain level. The stories that other people share about their journey and experiences can help you find out the mystery of your true self.

Enneagram Typing And Tests

This book was designed to give you a starting point toward finding out who you really are. With the help of the information, you are able to generate report on your behaviors, beliefs, and attitudes, and that would have been the data you use to type yourself. There is, however, a problem with self-reported data – the data that you yourself have collected about you.

The Pitfalls Of Using Self-Reported Data

Self-reported data is frequently used in psychological studies, of which personality analysis is a part, primarily because the information is easy to obtain. In fact, clinicians use self-reported data to an extent in order to make the right diagnosis – they ask questions. The main problem with self-reported data is that it has its limitations, such as the following:

Social Desirability Concerns – You might not want to admit certain undesirable traits about yourself so you refuse to acknowledge them, resulting to inaccurate data.

Question Order Bias – overtime, as the subject may react differently based on the other of in, which the questions appeared.

Introspective Ability – Some subjects lack the ability required to properly evaluate themselves. They might not be able to connect the dots or miss important things entirely.

Problems with the Interpretation of the questions – In some cases, the subject finds the wording of the questions confusing. Some people may also take a certain word differently.

Enneagram Typing Programs and Centers

Self-report data should not be the sole source of data if your goal is to be as accurate as possible. This is not to say you should not ever use self-reported data. However, it should be used in conjunction with other information such as the individual's actual behavior.

Third parties are not as close to you so they may be able to spot response biases. They have access to tools such as specially designed questionnaires that have been evaluated to make sure that they can produce consistent results over time.

You can always try the Enneagram tests you see online for fun, but do not forget that they may not always give accurate results due to the limitations of self-reported data. Some of them have been developed by Enneagram community members who have also just begun their journey.

How To Get Accurate Results When Taking An Enneagram Test

There are a few things to keep in mind when taking any Enneagram test to ensure that you get accurate results.

1. Make sure to answer the questions honestly. Ask yourself these questions before choosing an answer:

Is that really how you are?

Are you sure, it is not just something you would like to be?

Is that something you have tended to do so or to be in the past?

The answers to all those questions should be 'yes'.

It is difficult to answer many of the questions honestly, because it is human nature to want to see themselves as better than they are. That is why the Dunning-Kruger effect is so prevalent in human beings.

2. Keep in mind that your self-image is not your true image. We tend to have preconceived notions about ourselves, some of which are not true at all.

For example, you like to think of yourself as a naturally generous person, but it could be that your generosity is an effort to curb your fears of maintaining harmony. You tend to give way so much that you end up resentful but you do not believe that you truly are resentful.

To get accurate results from your Enneagram analysis, keep these natural tendencies in mind.

3. It might help to try to look from the outside.

When answering questions, consider if the answer you have chosen is how someone close to you would describe you as well.

After Getting the Results

There is one thing you should not stop doing after getting your results – learning. Find out more about your Type and examine the other types that also seem to be dominant in you.

Enneagram tests generally generate a report in which you get a score for each pf the nine types. Scoring the highest in a particular category indicates that you are likely dominant in that category. Learn more about the top three categories in which you got the highest scores.

More importantly, try to listen to other people's stories. Listen to what they have to say about their own journey to self-discovery. Learn about how a certain type lives his life, and how they cope with life's challenges. We can always learn from each other.

Eventually, you will see there is a pattern to everything – every action has its corresponding reaction and each one of is affected by the other.

Chapter 13: Elements Of Emotional Intelligence (Mixed Model By Goleman)

One of the most popular models of EI was developed by Daniel Goleman. The Mixed Model of EI focuses mainly on studying EI through the individuals' skills and competencies that affect performance in leadership roles. This is why Goleman's model of EI is typical in corporate and other professional settings. Goleman's Mixed Model of EI is highly suitable in the training and evaluation of individuals showing high potential for management roles.

Goleman's Mixed Model proposes that there are five important elements to Emotional Intelligence. Within each element of EI in the Mixed Model, Goleman outlined a set of emotional abilities which are now referred to as "hallmarks". These qualities are not a person's innate talents or personality characteristics, but rather capabilities that can be learned and enhanced to achieve heightened levels of performance. These five elements are:

Self-Awareness

Your self-awareness is your ability to recognize your own emotions, strengths and weaknesses, goals, what motivates you, and your values. This also includes your ability to recognize your effect on others; particularly how intuitive you are when it comes to influencing the emotions of others around you.

Definitive indications of your self-awareness would be your level of self-confidence, your most objective assessments of yourself, and your abilities for self-deprecating sense of humor.

Your self-awareness relies on your ability to monitor your own emotions and how accurately you are able to identify others' emotions.

Self-Regulation

Your ability for self-regulation involves how you recognize your own disruptive emotions (including your impulses) and how you control or channel these negative emotions to a more productive direction. How well do you think before you act and are you able to suspend judgment for later?

The hallmarks for your ability to self-regulate include your levels of trustworthiness and integrity, how comfortable you are with uncertainty, and how you embrace change.

Motivation

How you are able to motivate yourself towards the successful achievement of your own goals speaks to your own emotional intelligence, according to the Mixed Model. This includes both your practical goals (such as a raise or promotion at work) and your drive for achievement, per se. The Mixed Model is outlined to identify highly emotionally intelligent individuals who strive for success just for the sake of, well… succeeding.

Are you driven more by external rewards (such as money and status), or are you motivated by the more meaningful things in life such as joy, a natural desire to learn, or by the inward fulfillment that comes from being charitable? How persistent are you in pursuing these goals of yours?

The hallmarks of motivation would be how strong your drive to achieve is, your optimism in the face of defeat, and your commitment to the organizations you belong in.

Empathy

Empathy, in general terms, is your ability to understand and share in the feelings of others. Not to be confused with sympathy, which is feeling sorry for another person experiencing difficulties, empathy is more about being able to personally identify with the experience (or experiences) of another and taking the shared emotion into consideration in deciding how to relate to that other person.

How well do you understand the emotional makeup of others? Are you always able to treat other people appropriately, given their emotional states?

In the workplace, the hallmarks of empathy include expertise in developing and retaining talent, cultural sensitivity, and service to clients and customers. In the more generic context, empathy is often thought to encroach on, or lead to, sympathy, which involves concern or a desire to mitigate negative emotions or experiences in others. Take note, however, that empathy is not necessarily equivalent to compassion. Empathy can be employed for either compassionate or cruel behavior. Take, for instance, serial rapists who are able to attract only to eventually violate several partners -- they tend to have great empathic skills.

Otherwise, they would not have been able to draw victims close so easily.

Social Skills

This element of EI rides heavily on your abilities for self-awareness and self-regulation in the realm of your relationships with others. Are you able to persuade others into the direction you wish them to go? If you manage people at work, how creative are you in motivating your team members? In personal relationships, how well do you communicate your positive attributes and keep your friends or partner interested in being around you?

Are you able to manage your existing relationships without difficulty? Are you able to build rapport with others without much effort? The hallmarks of social skills are effectiveness in initiating change, persuasiveness, and the ability to build and lead a group.

The Mixed Model concurs that people are born with cognitive abilities and personality characteristics. And these inherent traits, unique to each individual, are highly instrumental in determining a person's potential for success when coupled with an active development of his or her emotional intelligence.

This is mainly why the Mixed Model of EI is highly popular in the business setting. Business organizations find the theories related to EI to be quite effective in maximizing their human resources. It is not uncommon for manpower-rich business organizations to perform evaluations of existing staff members or potential hires based on the Mixed Model's set of values. Gauging the EI levels of potential hires as early as in the recruitment stages and further developing current staff's EI will only serve any business' culture and, yes, bottom line well.

Chapter 14: The Investigator (Type 5)

Also known as the Observer or the Sage

Fifteen Signs You're An Investigator

You have an insatiable need to find out why things are the way they are - scientifically and otherwise.

You have a strong urge to question the status quo.

You feel that a day in which you haven't learned anything new is a day wasted.

If a subject or activity captures your interest, you focus your attention on it intently, until you have fully mastered it.

You might have been described by others - either to your face or otherwise! - as eccentric.

You hate being pressured into making quick decisions.

You are inclined to hold tension in your gut.

You might sometimes feel that you are "stuck" in your head and that it takes quite an effort to get back into your body.

You are not big on small talk. You find it uncomfortable and, quite frankly, a complete waste of time.

Your privacy is of the utmost importance to you and it is quite common for you to experience other people as intrusive.

You might feel the need to acquire knowledge and expertise in a bid to overcome deep-seated feelings of inadequacy and self-doubt.

You are highly likely to be an expert in your field and that field might be scholarly or highly technical.

You have a propensity to withdraw into the safety of your mind when life seems too threatening or overly demanding.

You are most probably well-read, not to mention thoughtful and intelligent.

It takes you a while to become comfortable with another person, but once you have achieved that level of comfort, you are a devoted companion and that friendship is likely to last a lifetime.

Do you think you might possibly be a Five?

The Inspector Overview

The Investigator spends a lot of time in his or her own head. This is a similarity they have with the Four, but while the Four's comfort zone is in the realm of the imagination and the emotions, the five exists comfortably in the intellect. The Inspector has the habit of retreating into the world of thought when life gets too much. This is their safe place, where they can prepare to face the outside world once again because they like to be prepared and absolutely hate to be put on the spot. They are afraid, in fact, that they don't have what it takes to fully face life.

The Investigator, as the name implies, is sometimes scientifically oriented, but they may also strive for excellence in the area of the humanities.

The type Five can come across as eccentric. This might have something to do with their refusal to bend their beliefs to conform to the mainstream opinion. Freedom of thought is of paramount importance to the Observer, but they can be shy and struggle when it comes to dealing with and expressing their emotions. For this reason, relationships can be difficult for the type Five. This will make them feel lonely at times. Their independent nature can also add to the challenge of relationships, both in the romantic sense, but also when it comes to accepting help from well-meaning people.

The Investigator can be quite a sensitive soul. This makes them feel vulnerable so they commonly adopt coping mechanisms to shield themselves. This can make them come across as intellectually arrogant or carelessly indifferent. This also doesn't help with relationships! But if you learn how to penetrate these barriers, you've got yourself a friend for life.

Because of their need for privacy and fear of intrusion, Fives usually disguise their very strong feelings. This disguise can be extremely effective. For some Fives, one of their biggest fears is of being overwhelmed, so they attempt to keep their lives as simple as possible, making few demands on others in the hope that they will have few demands made on them in return.

Historical or famous Fives of note include: Albert Einstein, Stephen Hawking, Vincent Van Gogh, Georgia O'Keefe, Emily Dickinson, Bill Gates, Eckhart Tolle, Alfred Hitchcock,The Buddha, Oliver Sacks, Edvard Munch, Friedrich Nietzsche, James Joyce, Jean-Paul Sartre, Stephen King, Salvador Dali, Agatha Christie, Mark Zuckerberg, Kurt Kobain, Peter Gabriel, Marlene Dietrich, Jodie Foster, Gary Larson, David Lynch, Tim Burton, Stanely Kubrick, Annie Liebovitz and Susan Sontag.

The Investigator Levels

Healthy

Visionary

The healthy Five is open-minded to the core. He or she can see the big picture while at the same time, appreciating and comprehending the minutiae. Their view of the world is visionary, seeing everything that can be improved for future generations and having some idea of how to make these improvements happen. They are the pioneers of the world; they are the scientists that make ground-breaking discoveries and the intellectuals that change the way we perceive the forces around us.

Observant

The healthy Five doesn't miss a thing. Their mental alertness is extraordinarily acute and their ability to focus and concentrate is second to none. They are perceptive and insightful with limitless curiosity. Their intellect is always seeking something new to sink its teeth into.

Expert

You will often find a five at the zenith of their chosen filed, as they have a seemingly unlimited capacity to attain mastery of whatever it is that interests them. They find knowledge wildly exciting and their passion often causes them to innovate and invent. Their work is often highly original and of great value to the world. The Investigator at this healthy level is frequently independent and possesses some marvellous idiosyncrasies.

Neutral

Conceptualizing

The Five will usually work everything out in their minds before acting on an idea. This allows them to fine tune everything from the outset. They love to be prepared and have all the required resources at their fingertips. They are studious and hard-working and often become specialists within their fields, while not being afraid to challenge the accepted way of doing things.

Detached

The Investigator, or the Observer, can sometimes become so involved in their intellectual world or the complex project on which they are working, that they become quite detached from reality. They lose touch with the real world, often in quite a disembodied way and become so preoccupied by their visions that matters such as relationships go by the wayside. At this point, the Five displays a kind of high-strung intensity and might even develop a fascination with offbeat or disturbing subjects.

Antagonistic

Beware of trying to interfere with the not-so-mature Five's interior world. They will not thank you for it! They will defend their personal vision at all costs, becoming aggressive and rude with those who oppose their - often radical - views.

Unhealthy

Reclusive

The shyness of an unhealthy Five can go into overdrive. Not only do they become isolated from other humans, but also from reality. Their eccentricity is no longer pleasant and their personality becomes increasingly unstable. They shun company and tend to live a hermit-like existence.

Obsessive

This is obsession in its most unhealthy form. Their ideas become threatening - even to themselves. The Investigator in this state is delusional and suffers from phobias.

Deranged

At the lowest possible level, we are in the area of schizotypal personality disorders. It is a dangerously self-destructive state and psychosis or suicide may be the end result.

The Investigator Wings

Type Five with a Four wing (5W4)

The influence of the Four wing on the Type Five personality can cause them to be more comfortable when it comes to expressing their emotions. They are still curious, reserved and perhaps a little more creative.

It should come as no surprise that the Type Five with a Four wing likes to be alone as both types in their purity enjoy alone time.

The strengths of the 5W4 include a capacity for deep attentiveness and the ability to observe and understand the most tiny details. They think and express themselves creatively and work well independently. But like everyone else, The Type Five with a Four wing is by no means perfect. He or she can be hyper-sensitive and also struggle, at times, to think in a practical and realistic way. They can be too self-absorbed and are prone to distancing themselves from other people.

If you need to communicate with an Investigator with a Five wing, you will do well to be as clear as possible and give them adequate time to process before pressing them for a response. If you are working with them, you would be advised to keep meetings to a minimum, be concise in your explanations and sensitive when giving feedback.

This variant of the Observer is energized by gaining knowledge, new skills and by being appreciated. They will feel drained if they have to spend too much time with other people or forced into situations that overwhelm them. And they certainly do not appreciate harsh criticism!

Type Five with a Six wing (5W6)

When the Six wing is dominant in the Type Five, the Investigator becomes more cooperative. Such a person will also be more inclined to use their impressive knowledge to solve problems rather than to intellectualize. This modification on the Five is inclined to be logical, independent and practical. They desire to be of use and to put their knowledge to work. They want to make the world a better place and feel more worthy in the process.

Their more positive traits include such qualities as focus and good organization, not to mention a passion for learning and improving. They often have a great capacity for solving complex problems and they are the type you want to have around in a crisis as they are adept at remaining calm.

However, the Type Five with a Six wing does have various blind spots. They can have difficulty relating to others and can be overly defensive in their wish to protect their privacy. They can come across as cold and aloof and need to be inspired in order to take any action.

This alternative Investigator loves to solve problems, especially when it makes them feel as if they are making a valuable contribution to society. Their pursuit of knowledge is enthusiastic, particularly when it comes to areas in which they are personally interested. They are drained by spending too much time around others and energized by spending time alone. Always be aware of their propensity for self-doubt in your dealings with them.

Advice for The Investigator

Stay in your body. Your intellect is a wonderful tool but it is also necessary to stay connected to other people and to the real world. An excellent way of doing this is by staying in touch with your body and your physical sensations through exercise.

Trust is an issue for a Five and because of this, they can find it very hard to open up to other people. When they experience conflict in a relationship, their natural tendency is to withdraw and isolate themselves. This is, of course, not particularly healthy behavior. The Investigator would do well to remember that conflicts are a normal part of every relationship and the appropriate course of action is to work things out.

It is tough for Type Five on The Enneagram to relax. This is because of their innate intensity. It is therefore important for the Five to devise ways to wind down that are suitable and appropriate. Meditation, yoga and running are all recommended.

The Five can lose his or her sense of perspective and quite easily feel overwhelmed as there are so many factors to consider! To help you make an accurate assessment in these circumstances, seek out the advice of someone you trust (after first working on your trust issues)!

Be selective in the projects you choose to become involved with. Make sure that they are life-affirming and take you in the direction in which you want to go. Make sure you are not distracting yourself in an unworthy way and wasting your precious time.

Chapter 15: Enneagram Type 3: The Performer

Also known as the Achiever, the Performer is the third type of personality within the Enneagram. They follow their own motivations and desires, making them particularly unique, even amongst the other personality types. They are adaptable and driven toward success, while also being charming and attractive—their own confidence can be enticing for others. They are quite competent and driven by their own ambition while also able to remain poised and diplomatic. They, like Perfectionists, tend to get caught up in workaholic behavior. However, at their best, they are role models.

Overview of the Performer

Characteristic Role: Performer

Ego fixation: Vanity

Holy idea: Hope and the law
Basic fear: Worthlessness
Basic desire: Feeling valuable
Temptation: Pushing oneself toward perfection
Vice: Deceit
Virtue: Truthfulness and authenticity

Direction of disintegration: Type 9: The Mediator

Direction of integration: Type 6: The Loyal Skeptic

The Performer is quite unique, and the defining characteristics of this personality type include:

Being strongly aware and in touch with social norms and niceties

Able to accomplish nearly anything with their tenacity and ambition

They are often on-the-go and constantly busy

They usually have packed schedules as a sign of their ambition

They may enjoy acting, but this can vary from person to person

They are largely charismatic, and they make excellent first impressions while maintaining an outer image of being persuasive

A Snapshot of the Performer

The Performer, in particular, is quite sophisticated and will always come across as polished and like they have everything in order, even if that could not be further from the truth. They are able to engage in near-endless levels of productivity, and they will endlessly strive toward achieving those goals that they have, despite their high standards—and they will meet them. They are nearly as perfectionistic as the Perfectionists, needing to be seen as smart, ambitions, and the best at everything they do. They wish to be remembered for what they have done, and they want to make an impact that everyone recognizes and acknowledges. They are usually busy nearly constantly, with their schedules bursting full of time for both fun and business, keeping them occupied. This is for the best—they love to keep themselves moving toward their goals, and they are constantly admired for their energy and tenacity toward pursuing those goals.

The Performer's Values

The three key values in the Performer's life are recognition, accolades, and status. They have that Type-A personality that keeps them on the edge of their seat and constantly striving for better. They are all about self-improvement as they achieve their goals and get the recognition that they desire. Above all else, however, they want to be productive. They value checking things off their to-do list more than anything else, and they find that if they spend too much time planning or attempting to figure out what to do, they have wasted time. They would rather be action-oriented, even if they have to go back and make some corrections after the fact, so long as they are able to keep themselves busy.

Recognizing the Performer

When you want to recognize the Performer, simply look for the one that everyone admires—this individual is able to not only get everything on their massive to-do list done before their deadlines, but they can do so while looking good to boot. They are able to manage their image with ease, balancing it with their own productivity, and in doing so, they are able to ensure that they look worthy of the admiration that they are seeking.

These people always seem to know exactly what to say and how to make friends. They seem to have the perfect life, typically lining up closely with their gender norms, and they will always have a plan. If you ask where they will be in ten years, they will tell you—as well as how they plan to get there.

The Performer and Health

The Healthy Performer

At optimal health, the Performer is driven and kind. They have the drive of the Perfectionist with the kindness of the Giver. They are able to help those around them when needed, and it never seems to be a drain on them. They are able to push people into new territories, bettering everyone and everything they touch. They are able to engage with others charismatically and push other people with their ideas, and everyone is happy to hear them out. They are quite adaptable, and all of this together makes them incredibly successful in the workplace. They are not only good at work, either—they are friendly, playful, and witty, and this allows for the healthy Performer to have the perfect balance between their work and life balance.

The Average Performer

The average Performer is often a busybody who is constantly seeking for ways to stay engaged. They are always seeking out new goals that they can get through, as well as how to look their best with ease. They want to make sure that they are able to get through their day with as much attention as they deserve, and they are constantly seeking out new projects or new networks to keep. They constantly fill up their schedules, and as they fill, the fear of failure drives them forward, keeping them motivated and working. They may become obsessed over social media, using it as an easy way to compare where they are to where other people are, and in doing so, they can grow arrogant, especially if they are posting about themselves. They must be in first place at all times, and they will feel threatened if they are not.

The Unhealthy Performer

When unhealthy, the Performer becomes quite jealous. They will see everything as a competition, and because of their nature and need to be at the top, they will constantly focus on one-upping those around them that they feel are their competition. They will constantly be seeking out approval from other people, and when they do not get that, they can start to shut down or grow depressed. This slows them down, and their motivation disappears, further leading to lower self-esteem. They feel like a hollow shell, feeling like the image they worked so hard to promote has been destroyed. At their worst, they may even begin to backstab and manipulate others, destroying other reputations with their own in an attempt to benefit themselves.

The Performer's Strengths

Physical: The Performer is able to master the art of slowing down when needed, allowing them to feel grounded and balanced instead of constantly on the go—they are able to give themselves time for self-discovery and self-care

Emotional: They are able to let go of that need for a superior self-image in order to accept their own weaknesses as well—they are able to realize that it is okay to have weaknesses and those weaknesses do not define them as people or take away their worth

Mental: They are able to be quite achieved and charismatic, able to use their drive to keep themselves developing and constantly striving for better at all costs—they can get past mediocrity and discover their own greatness

Relational: They are able to inspire others to get past the status quo, striving for more and better, proving to others that they should always be aiming for excellence instead of competence

Spiritual: They are able to rediscover their veracity—their devotion to the truth

The Performer's Weaknesses

Physical: The Performer tends to become hyper-focused on physical appearance and may overcompensate in order to achieve the desired body. They may exercise too much or starve themselves in order to lose weight—they are at risk for addiction to stimulants

Emotional: They are typically caught up in negative emotions such as shame, guilt, vanity, and even jealousy thanks to their competitive nature, and this can lead to selfishness, callousness, and even impatience. They are also prone to narcissism, as well as feeling empty and worthless

Mental: Because they are constantly striving to be the best, they sometimes get caught up in thinking that they are superior to other people, making it clear to others and that it is not okay to make any mistakes, leading to a hyper-focus on perfectionism

Relational: They feel like relationships become problematic when those around them are not driven the same way they are—when they see that others are not trying to be as ambitious, they may instead become manipulative to get those around them to pick up the slack

Spiritual: When out of touch with their spiritual self, they can feel like they are worthless, causing their ego to cope with an image of success, even though they feel like they are a failure—they become deceptive

The Performer in a Relationship

In this relationship, you will find that the other party is likely going to want and need recognition—you can provide this through having a regard for the Performer rather than his or her behaviors. Keep in mind as well that the Performer has a tendency to get caught up in the middle between what an idea about an emotion is and actually feeling it—they have a tendency to feel what is thought, so if they think that they are stupid, they will feel that they are stupid, for example.

When you are in a relationship with a Performer, keep in mind that you need to be entirely present when they present their emotions to you—they want the validation from you, and they will likely struggle as they are communicating about the emotions in the first place. As the emotions start to lean toward darker as well, you may find that they will entirely reject the idea of negative feedback that they disagree with—they will not see it as worthy of attention, and if this arises, try discussing the feedback as a learning experience that can help them become better. They are also likely to rush forward during negative emotions, almost as if they can outpace them.

Keep in mind that, above all, a Performer in a relationship wants a connection—they want you to share how you are feeling with them, and you should always make it a point to tell them when you feel like they are not making time for you. They do want time to spend connecting with you, but it can be difficult to manage that time when they are so busy chasing after all their end goals, as well.

Chapter 16: The Third Personality

As a beginner in the world of Enneagram, these different and diverse personalities might sound a bit strange to you. If this is the case, there is no need to panic. It is completely normal. I was once in your shoes, years ago, when I was first getting started. But as I learned more and began to identify the various personality traits that I possess, it all began to fall into place.

So, you don't identify with either the reformer or lover personalities? Perhaps you are more of an Achiever. Now, I know, you are probably asking who these Achievers are. This is the third personality trait we will look at. Other names given to them are; result-oriented, success-driven, pragmatic, and adaptable. They are given these names because of their need for success in various endeavors. Whatever field they find themselves in, they strive for success in order to build their level of self-worth.

The description of the Achievers

People with this kind of personality are typically described as charming, energetic, attractive, and elegant. In whatever they do, their competence drives them to excellence. Where many people would usually be nonchalant about development and class, achievers are always conscious of it. They are incredibly diplomatic and tactical in their approach to things because their concern is to achieve success all the time.

In the mind of an achiever, failure is essentially the worst thing on earth, which is precisely why they would use all their power to hit every challenge to achieve the desired results; success. Things that could draw achievers back while aiming at a particular challenge are their concerning thoughts on how people will perceive them and the kind of image that they might portray. Because of their drive to succeed, people with these traits, have an incredibly competitive mind, and those who can work all the time are their greatest threat. In fact, they would, by all means, avoid them because they feel that they create a kind of stress for them. In some ways, achievers dealing with competition is equivalent to them beating the shadows of themselves. Achievers are also a source of good inspiration to the people around them.

They are scared of being irrelevant and worthless. They also try to be the best at doing a particular thing; they always want to retain that position no matter the circumstances. They will go to any length in order to achieve their success. All that they want is to be valuable and worthy of everything in their name. They avoid any kind of venture that is likely to fail because this would hurt them very badly.

It isn't as though they wouldn't attempt a new venture, but whatever they decide to try has to be something they are sure to succeed at. People with this personality trait are professionals at everything they do. Achievers always want to be confirmed as the best especially if people doubt how excellent they could they could be a something. They often stand out from the crowd with great distinction. Most importantly, achievers want attention.

They work best when receiving praise as opposed to condemnation. Admiration is part of what drives achievers in whatever they do –people must admire excellence. Funny enough, achievers don't just work for people, they want to impress them. No matter how trivial that thing is, achievers are always out to impress others, especially those in a supervisory role. When they do not get recognition, they can be dejected for days. The majority of people who fall into this personality type will not feel like working anymore and want to resign. This is their weakness; rejection from people.

The name given to this category is premised on the fact that these people can aim at anything in life and achieve success. Because of their achievements, many people look up to them as models of the human race. This is actually their aim too. They are aware of the contribution of humans to the world, so they do everything to develop themselves and also to motivate people around them.

Achievers are always selected as representatives of people wherever they find themselves. Many people take it as goodwill to use achievers as the representatives because of excellence, motivation, and achievements. Some of them have been leading their class from childhood. They wouldn't force it; it is what people want. Achievers are always the standout and leader of the group.

The achievers are regarded as the most loved among other types of the Enneagram personalities. They are the role models for a lot of people of their own enneagram personality and the other eight as well. They are living legends because of their records which have to fend them the social value they desire. They spend most of their time doing what they can do best. With this development, many are given adequate inspiration to build themselves, as their mentors are doing so too.

There is this special thing about the achievers: attaining success based on what their communities call it. In one place, being successful could be tied to having material things such as cars, houses, etc. In another place, it could be the ability to birth great and feasible ideas. Whatever the prerequisites, achievers will always get their desire, success. They still want to leave a legacy of success behind them; this is part of their drive.

Even when achievers are young, they love to focus on those impossible things they met as history in order to beat it and lead among their families. No matter the price of being the best and of excellence, the achievers are ready to pay it. They can't just be anybody without a name. Most of them are reckoned within their communities, nations, states, and countries. When their names are mentioned, they save lives and properties. Achievers will surely buy affluence for their families, both nuclear and extended. They are the heroes of our time, and most times, their achievement records are unbeatable. This is their goal.

Achievers do not aim for success for any reason other than their fear of been forgotten after their death. They put everything together to be remembered forever in their residence. There is no special dividend expected from the people achievers are helping; they just want them to proclaim their names around the world. People must speak of their achievements and prowess through the ages.

A lot of people with the "achiever" personality trait, are quite addicted to some things because of their success orientation and drive. They can starve themselves when on the mission of achievement. They hardly take time to rest, and they work till their body is completely exhausted. Some of them get addicted to drugs such as cocaine, to stimulate themselves. Whatever the addiction, they barely see it as bad once they attain the fame they want.

There are great people known for this kind personality. They might not have been, entirely, bearing this personality but have a touch of it. Some of them are Bill Clinton, Justin Bieber, Courtney Cox, Michael Jordan, Augustus Caesar, Werner Erhard, Paul McCartney, Whitney Houston, Reese Witherspoon, Richard Gere, Dick Clark, Chef Daniel Boulud, Tony Robbins, Ken Watanabe, etc.

There is nothing without its disadvantages; the same applies to the achiever personality. They face a few challenges given below:

The tendency to lose themselves

Achievers desire to be the best in spite of all odds. With this desire, they tend to lose their authentic self because they leave out very little time to take care of themselves. They are subject to the deception of fame and achievement. Usually, because achievers tend to chase glory from their childhood, they lose themselves even before they know themselves. This is so sad, but it's the truth.

Lack of feeling

Achievers are purely active people; they barely have time for feelings. It is as bad as not paying attention to whatever is happening around them. They don't have or hardly feel people's emotions. It is as if their feelings have separated from them. When things happen to them, they appear to be numbed and barely take it the way other people do. So far, their achievements are attained; whatever negative feelings were induced scarcely concerns them.

Lack of focus

Many achievers don't really know what they want. All they do is to satisfy the desires of others. Their numbed attitudes towards feelings could be because they believe that since they would enjoy the gain, they should endure the pain too. Achievers don't have a great focus; they only want achievements and records. Their aim for fame blinds their eyes.

Having stated the possible challenges of achievers, it is necessary to give some ways to overcome these challenges. Achievers could develop and grow in the following few ways:

Create and accept your own needs and feeling

To grow as an achiever, you have to learn how to succumb to your feelings. Whenever you're exhausted, be truthful to yourself; take enough time to rest. The achievements that you're always running after are not equivalent to your life. People wouldn't love you less simply because you took some time off. Avoid faking your feelings. You are human, and it is normal to get tired.

Learn how to give yourself time

This isn't saying that you should neglect your goals and sleep all day; it merely means that you need to take time to regain strength and not exhaust yourself. You would be surprised what a thirty-minute nap would do for you. You should also practice taking things slow and taking time to think things through. Take enough rest and achieve your dreams; nobody is in competition with you; after all, they can't understand your own approach.

Resist doing the acceptable

Achievers always want to do things that are acceptable to others at their own detriment. It is about time you resisted the feeling to please people and focus on your needs. This is critical to living a happy life. Sometimes, it is fine not to do things that will satisfy people. As long as it doesn't hurt anyone adversely, do things you want to do because you want to do them.

Strengthen your relationships

If you must exhaust yourself in order to meet your goals, try to take out time to discuss and strengthen your relations with the people in your life. You can't always tell everyone you're busy all the time. Your family and friends should get some of your time too. You will do this consciously by giving yourself the time to work and also devote time to your friends and family. Remember that both your death and life are affected by them. Give them your life before they have to accept your death.

Work on your own goals

Usually, the achiever's fame comes from helping others with their plans. The truth is that when you work on your personal goals, you have more chances of earning better achievements. By doing so, you will achieve not only fame but also happiness that comes from the fulfillment of your goals. A real legacy is achieved when your life's work was for you and not someone else. This is what could be referred to as an achievement.

In conclusion, achievers are one of the best of the enneagram personalities and ironically, suffer more than the others as well. They're true heroes. Nevertheless, there is always time for everything. Time to be everyone's hero and also time to watch out for yourself. What is the gain of an achiever if he or she saves the day and ends up losing his or herself? Thus, as an achiever, you need to be steadfast, you need to be cautious, and you need to be thoughtful too. That is the only way you can achieve real success in the world. The next chapter promises to be much more captivating and intriguing. Stay with us as we unravel the next personality trait – the Individualist.

Conclusion

Enneagram can be well thought-out as a tool which can be used to find the personality outlines of different persons belongs to different areas and cultures. Other tools are also available for example Myers- Briggs profile or DISC, but the Enneagram provides the 9 different personality types which is far better than them. Discovering the exact personality types by using the Enneagram test is the start of the personality discovery. The journey is not end here because after this first step when one can well aware of his personality type using these tests, one has to analyze different personality types to know the nature of the relationships among them. The Enneagram expose important span of relationships and assists in better understanding what drives and motivates relationships in between different types as well as the impact that they have on relationships. In exploring the Enneagram and getting to know approximately our favored kind, we study greater about ourselves, about the gifts and obstacles of our type, and approximately the possible nature of our relationships with others. As we have explained in advance, none of those are absolutes – they're indicators. But they offer us with records and insights which we will then use to develop ourselves and boom our emotional health.

www.ingramcontent.com/pod-product-compliance
Lightning Source LLC
Chambersburg PA
CBHW072005070526
44583CB00015B/1338